FAITH: THE SUBSTANCE
OF THINGS UNSEEN

Discovering
Deeper Faith
and
True Intimacy
with God

Faith: THE SUBSTANCE OF THINGS UNSEEN

Penelope J. Stokes

Tyndale House Publishers, Inc.
WHEATON, ILLINOIS

All Scripture quotations, unless otherwise indicated, are taken from the *Holy Bible,* New International Version®. Copyright © 1973, 1978, 1984 by International Bible Society. Used by permission of Zondervan Publishing House. All rights reserved. The "NIV" and "New International Version" trademarks are registered in the United States Patent and Trademark Office by International Bible Society. Use of either trademark requires permission of International Bible Society.

Scripture quotations marked NRSV are taken from the New Revised Standard Version of the Bible, copyrighted, 1989 by the Division of Christian Education of the National Council of the Churches of Christ in the United States of America, and are used by permission. All rights reserved.

Scripture quotations marked NASB are taken from the *New American Standard Bible,* © 1960, 1962, 1963, 1968, 1971, 1972, 1973, 1975, 1977 by The Lockman Foundation. Used by permission.

Scripture quotations marked KJV are taken from the *Holy Bible,* King James Version.

Epigraphs by T. S. Eliot are taken from *The Four Quartets,* in *The Complete Poems and Plays of T. S. Eliot* (New York: Harcourt, Brace, & World, Inc., 1971).

Library of Congress Cataloging-in-Publication Data

Stokes, Penelope J.
  Faith: the substance of things unseen : discovering deeper faith and true intimacy with God / Penelope J. Stokes.
    p.   cm.
  ISBN 0-8423-1981-6 (softcover)
  1. Christian life. 2. Faith. I. Title.
BV4501.2.S7773   1995   94-40265
248.4—dc20

Printed in the United States of America

00 99 98 97 96
6   5   4   3   2   1

TO MY SKIN HORSES . . .

The people who loved God
and took the risk
to teach me
that a Stuffed Rabbit
could also become
Real

CONTENTS

ACKNOWLEDGMENTS

Special thanks are due to some extraordinary people who have made a profound impact upon my life and writing:

- ~ To my parents, Jim and Betty Stokes, who gave me both roots and wings . . .
- ~ To Charette Barta, the first to be touched by Quester's journey . . .
- ~ To LaVonne Neff, who shared the vision for this book . . .
- ~ To Jackie Ziemer, whose uncommon intimacy with God inspires me . . .

and

- ~ To Cindy Maddox, whose integrity, faith, and sense of humor keep me anchored in reality . . .

You have helped me through the dark times and shared in the glory.

This is a book about faith.

Not the white-knuckled, hang-on-till-you-die kind of persistence that often masquerades as spiritual strength, but real-life faith, the kind that gives us the courage to risk and reach out when our knees tremble and our heart fails us, when the road is dark and we haven't the faintest idea which way to go.

We begin with a premise—an important one: that life is not always easy, that the path is not always clear. We begin with an assumption—a basic one: that God loves us and desires what is best for us.

This is a book about the journey . . . about the process . . . about the ways God leads us into a deeper level of commitment, into a life of greater strength, into a daily experience of difficult challenges and lovely surprises.

Our journey begins with the parable of Quester, a woman who has lived all her life within the serenity of her parents' home, a stone fortress surrounded by a walled garden. Life is pleasant enough here, and certainly safe. There are no challenges, no dangers; all the answers are provided in the books Quester reads. She should be satisfied.

But she longs for more. And then she hears a Voice calling to her in the night, urging her to leave the safety of the walled garden to come out into the forest, to explore the world beyond the wall. . . .

Each of us has a walled garden, a fortress-home that provides safety and comfort, an insular place of protection where the answers are well defined. For many of us, that fortress is the church. We have accepted the definitive answers we have been taught; we wear the mantle of religion, fulfilling our parents' expectations, conforming to the unspoken attitudes of our friends. And our faith, as far as it goes, is genuine. The problem is, sometimes it doesn't go deep enough to satisfy the unspoken inner longings of our soul.

God has designed us for fellowship; the Bible calls the universal church the body of Christ. The local church, as a representative of the body, is intended to be a community of mutual nurturing and encouragement, a place of preparation, a launching pad for ministry to those around us.

The church can be all of that for us—and more. But sometimes it's not.

Sometimes the religious community gets so caught up in itself—in maintaining the status quo, in being popular or prophetic—that it fails to encourage and empower individual believers in their faith walk.

Sometimes we suspect that the really important questions aren't being asked at all.

And then we are faced with a difficult dilemma: to stay within the womb of safety, or to push our way out into the dangers of the unknown.

There is nothing innately wrong with being comfortable within the church, of course. We were created for community, and we share similar experiences. We cannot abandon organized religion and strike out entirely on our own.

But in our individual journeys of the spirit, we must go beyond *what we have been taught* to explore *who we are* in Christ. If our faith is to be authentic and personal, it must be tried in the crucible of reality. As the old spiritual says, "I must walk this lonesome valley . . . nobody else can walk it for me. . . ."

The spiritual pilgrimage is a journey into reality.

The church today often tells us — by implication, if not by direct dogma — that the individual's journey of faith is an upward, ever-increasing ascent from glory unto glory. From the cradle we are taught that Jesus answers all our questions, solves all our problems, gives us victory in all our battles.

Tragically, this teaching of the "victorious Christian life" rarely coincides with the reality of daily experience. We struggle with sin and stress. We question, and our questions remain largely unanswered. We pray, and our prayers often seem to go unheard. We try hard, yet our chronic sins abound.

Occasionally, we experience a moment of miracle — a split second of insight when the clouds around us open and we see the sunlight of God's face and feel the warmth of the Spirit's presence. Once in a while, we know that lightning flash of power when God's gracious intervention redeems us from ourselves or our circumstances; our prayers are answered, and we bask in the glory.

But the clouds inevitably close in again, and the blessing/curse of human memory begins to work against us. We remember the flashes of glory and believe, because we have been taught to believe it, that the splendor is the norm—the natural, expected state in which the believer is supposed to live.

Like Peter at the Transfiguration, we collect lumber and hammer and nails and draw up a blueprint for the house we intend to build upon the Mount of Glory. And when Jesus points a directive finger toward the valley and commands us to return to the shadowlands, we are dismayed, disappointed—even despairing.

We blame ourselves: If we just had more faith, we could live forever in the afterglow of Christ's radiance. If we could get our mind off the daily struggles of earthly existence, we could know the uninterrupted joy of God's presence.

Thus we are taught; and thus, to the detriment of our faith, we believe.

Yet the Bible, and the lives of the saints, clearly indicate that the journey of the faithful is not a leisurely stroll along paths of light. With the hope of redemption held out before them, our first parents nevertheless faced a wilderness of sin and struggle on their way to the Resurrection, a journey bounded on both ends by the murder of an innocent.

Abraham, the father of faith, was led out "not knowing where he was going." Indeed, if he had known, he might have refused. After all, he was called upon to witness his own kinsman's defection to the world's system; he became the father of nations, but not before he had attempted to fulfill God's purposes in his own way—by fathering Ishmael. The Lord fulfilled the impossible promise in the birth of Isaac, but then called upon

Abraham to do the unthinkable—to offer that promised son upon an altar of sacrifice.

Throughout the history of the church, men and women have been called to make their journey along "a way they do not know." Moses finally got his people to the Promised Land, only to discover that the land of milk and honey also overflowed with giants. Although Augustine, in his heart of hearts, was drawn to God, still he prayed, "Lord, make me chaste—but not yet." St. John of the Cross agonized through the dark night of the soul. Brother Lawrence, even while practicing the presence of God, still had his pots and pans to scrub.

The journey of the spirit is not a highway for saints and mystics, but an ordinary path laid out for ordinary people. All of us have a call to answer; all of us have a road of faith to walk. And while each of us has individual stumbling points and places of darkness, we share in a single truth: that the *process* is of supreme importance to the Lord. And the process of moving from religion to reality is a way that leads to true intimacy with God.

PART ONE

The Voice from beyond the Wall

Quester stood with one hand on the gate latch. Her fingers trembled.

She looked over her shoulder. Behind her rose the great fortress-house that had been her home for as long as she could remember. Before her lay . . . what? She had no way of knowing, until she opened the gate and walked through to the other side.

A recurring dream had brought her here, a sleep crowded with beckoning paths and a low Voice calling her name. Even in the great stone house, invincible for generations, she found no rest. Even in the thousand books that lined the library walls, she found no answers.

A melancholy yearning had risen in her, a deep spring

fever of the heart. Unable to define the desire, uncertain what her soul was seeking, she had languished in a vague, ambivalent regret.

Then the Voice last night had stirred the ancient longing once again. *Come out, Quester,* it whispered. *There is much you have not seen.* Perhaps the questions would be answered, the nameless wish fulfilled, if she would venture out.

And so she stood at the single gate in the high-walled garden that surrounded the tower where she slept. Her parents were dead; the servants who cared for her in childhood all were gone; the tutor of her youth had, years ago, taken another charge and moved away. There was no one left to tell her not to go. But even as her hand trembled on the gate latch, she heard her mother's warning echoing in her mind: *Stay within the garden wall: Danger waits in the woods beyond.*

Quester was a good child, an obedient girl, and she had stayed within the boundaries, where she belonged. There was safety within the walls. Safety, but no answers. The questions still nagged at her, invading her dreams, filling her waking moments with fantasies of the world beyond the wall.

Never in all her years had Quester disobeyed her

mother's directive. She had fulfilled her parents' expectations, and in her own way, she trusted the impenetrability of her fortress-home. But something was missing. She believed what she had been taught, but she had never *experienced* life for herself.

The time had come to find her own answers.

She took a deep breath and pushed the gate open.

Quester had never dreamed of anything so beautiful, so full of life and color. There were woods as far as the eye could see, blooming wildflowers and pink crab trees; she caught a glimpse of rabbits in the bracken and a deer browsing just beyond an immense live oak. She was overwhelmed by the desire to go farther.

Following a curving path protected by a canopy of arching tree limbs, she made her way deeper and deeper into the forest. For hours she ambled along, breathing in the scent of wild primroses and lily of the valley. Sunlight dappled the leaves overhead and spilled liquid gold onto the path at her feet. Squirrels chattered in the trees, and one brave little chipmunk came almost close enough to touch. This was, indeed, a place of unknown delights.

Then, almost without warning, the forest began to grow dark. The sun had set, and Quester had no idea where she was. Panicked, she turned and began to retrace the path back to the safety of the garden.

She stumbled as she ran, trying to see through the gathering darkness in the woods before her. She was losing the path in the dim light.

Quester turned and looked behind her. Night was coming on fast, and the sounds of the forest began to close in around her. She retreated, groping through the underbrush. The way had seemed so obvious when she had set out earlier that morning; the woods benign, smelling of musk and wetness from the previous night's storm. Now the forest took on a menacing countenance, the shadowy face of an enemy waiting to attack around the next dark bend.

Now that she stood beyond the wall, all her mother's warnings came back to her. The trees faded into ominous shadows as the light dimmed; the last glimmer died in the west, and mysterious sounds of moving creatures began to stir in the forest. The path had disappeared, and Quester was afraid. Exhausted, she leaned against a tree, put her head on her knees, and wept.

CHAPTER ONE

The Nameless Longing

Footfalls echo in the memory
Down the passage which we did not take
Towards the door we never opened
Into the rose garden.
— T. S. ELIOT

I remember, on a springtime afternoon nearly twenty years ago, driving my car down a rutted country lane. The trees hung over the road, forming an arch, a breathing canopy, a living tunnel stretching as far as I could see. I can still remember the glorious ache in the pit of my stomach as my gaze took in the vibrancy of the redbud trees and the fragile beauty of the dogwoods, blooming wild and unattended in the virgin woods. It made me want to run away, to drive down that endless country road into the sunset and never return again.

Spring fever?

Perhaps. But the distant memory of that moment stirs longings in me even today. A certain fragrance, the flash of white blossoms in the trees along a very different roadside, can instantly transport me to that afternoon so long ago. Immediately, and with such vitality that it takes my breath away, I am twenty-four again. Twenty-four, with the future stretching out before me like that endless gravel road, limitless in its possibilities, hiding adventure beyond every shaded turn.

We have all felt it, that vague restlessness, that nameless longing that calls us toward the intriguing, slightly dangerous lure of the Great Unknown.

And we wonder: *What if . . . ?*

What if my life had taken a different turn—if I had married rather than remaining single . . . if I had chosen a different career . . . if I had learned a little earlier how to protect myself against the battering storms of life . . . if I had found out sooner what is really important to me?

What if I had taken the risk?

And the ultimate question: *Is it too late now?*

All of us, from childhood on, feel that tugging in our soul. We hear the Voice calling to us, *Come out; there is much you have not seen.*

In the process of growing up, sometimes the Voice is stilled, shut out by the responsibilities of adulthood, by our commitments to husband or wife, by the needs of our children, by the demands of our jobs and the incessant clamor of our daily duties.

But the longing still is there.

God put it there.

God's is the Voice that calls to us in the late hours of the night, when at last the bedlam around us has stilled. *Come out,* the Spirit whispers. *There is much you have not seen.*

If I am honest with myself, I know the truth of those words. The world around me may view me as mature, controlled, professional; but inside, in the secret places of my soul, I am filled with unanswered longings. There is much I have not seen.

And I am not alone.

From the moment of Creation, humankind has felt that pull toward discovery, the tugging of the heart toward that which we have not seen. And God answers that need in us. To Adam and Eve the Lord issued the call, "Come out and walk with me." God showed them new and wonderful things — a garden of delight, a world of abundance to discover, to name, to possess, to rule, to enjoy.

God offers the same to you, to me . . . to all of us.

But the way of discovery is not without its dangers. At the center of the garden of bliss stands a moment of decision. Like our first parents, we also face the choice to obey, even in the midst of our exploration — or to be lured from obedience by the seductive fragrance of forbidden knowledge.

THE DILEMMA OF THE TREE

The temptation to eat from the Tree of the Knowledge of Good and Evil is a powerful one; it is the temptation to go our own way, to find a path that suits us, to divorce ourselves from the guiding hand of the One who has called us out.

The dilemma of the Tree has been with us for centuries. Mystics and theologians, as well as ordinary people of faith like you and me, have pondered the question: Why did

God allow it? Why did the Almighty give Adam and Eve the choice to obey or to rebel?

This crucial question has become a focal point of all of religious history. And the answer, perhaps, lies finally and unfathomably in the mystery of God's own character. God lets us choose because God loves us, because true love is reciprocal, because response without freedom is nothing more than manipulation.

The Tree, after all, produced exactly the results promised by the tempter: Adam and Eve *did* receive the knowledge of good and evil. But it was a deceptive fulfillment. As Milton puts it in *Paradise Lost*, they learned of good and evil by finding "good lost, and evil got." And from that day forward, all of us have suffered from the effects of their decision.

THE GOD WHO CALLS

Why, then, if the danger was so great, did God put the Tree in the center of Paradise? Why did the Lord give them leave to wander freely—even allowing them to tend the Tree, as they did all the other trees in the Garden? Why does God continue to give us such freedom—to call us out into the world of exploration and discovery, to allow us to come so close to the agent of our own destruction?

From my own parents I learned why.

When I was very small—five or six, perhaps—my parents gave me a bicycle for Christmas. It was a magnificent machine, bright green with chrome fenders and a white leather seat. I loved that bicycle. It was my ticket to freedom.

Then one day—as children will do—I pulled an incredibly stupid stunt. I perched at the top of the highest hill on the block, took my hands off the handlebars, and went tearing down the incline at breakneck speed.

I had seen my older brother do this, and I couldn't let him get the best of me. Besides, I thought it must be a great thrill, rather like riding the rickety old roller coaster at the fair.

It was a thrill, all right. With the wind whipping my face and my legs stuck straight out to both sides and my ponytail lashing out behind me, it was the next best thing to flying.

Until I got to the bottom of the hill.

There the road made a sharp right turn onto the main street. I didn't get my hands onto the handlebars in time, or my feet onto the brakes. With a jolt my shiny new green-and-silver bike made a leap across the road into the ditch, and then I found out what flying was *really* like.

Like a clown shot out of a cannon, I made a high arc past the shrubbery and over Ginger, the neighbor's Chesapeake Bay retriever, to land in an ignominious heap just short of the concrete driveway.

The whole world, it seemed, came running to view my defeat. When at last it was determined that I had no broken bones, no serious injury except a critically wounded pride, my father said, "The next time you come down the hill, use your hands. And keep your feet on the brakes."

Perhaps it is a miracle that any of us ever grow up to be adults. Given the hair-raising risks of childhood, by rights we should all be dead before reaching the age of accountability. But parents who love their children know that they cannot—indeed, *must* not—protect them from every possible danger.

Protection must be commensurate with age and maturity. A toddler must be kept away from the stove and the butcher knives. But if toddlers become teenagers without learning how to handle fire or sharp instruments, they may grow into very hungry adults.

A certain amount of danger is inevitable, even desirable, in the process of maturing. As we grow up, we face the pain of a broken bone, the blood drawn by a playground cut, the death of a puppy under the wheels of an oncoming truck. We learn to deal with illness, battered hearts, and unrequited love. And so, gradually, we become adults, able to face the reality of a world gone terribly wrong, a world bent and broken by sin.

Like our earthly parents, God does not remove us from every source of danger or temptation. The Lord calls us forth to explore, to learn, to grow, to create, to become. If we are to become men and women of faith, we must realize that the way may not be easy, or even well marked. We do not always know where we are going.

And God does not always tell us.

The Unknown Land

The Bible is filled with examples of men and women who listened to the Voice calling to them from beyond the safety of their walled gardens, saying to them, *Come out*. And some of the callings were nothing short of outrageous.

The Voice that called to Noah instructed him in a

decidedly unusual venture. He was to build a boat, an enormous seaworthy barn — on dry land, in the midst of a society of people who had never seen rain! And when God shut the door on Noah and his family and their floating zoo, Noah had no way of knowing where they would set down or what they would find when the doors were opened again.

Abraham, certainly, is the prime biblical example of a person called out: "By faith Abraham, when called to go to a place he would later receive as his inheritance, obeyed and went, even though he did not know where he was going" (Hebrews 11:8).

Perhaps if Abraham had known, he would have resisted the call, for his life from that point on became a trial of his faith. Yet he clung tenaciously to God's promises, even when their fulfillment seemed impossible.

Down through history the call rang out: to Joseph, who saw the nameless longing take shape in his dreams and lead him into the land of Egypt; to Ruth, who left her own people to follow a bitter, heartbroken mother-in-law back to her homeland; to Esther, who gave up her heritage to become consort to a king; to Samuel, the child-prophet who heard the Voice whisper to him in the stillness of the night; to a barely grown girl named Mary, whose obedience to the Voice resulted in the promised incarnation of the one called Immanuel, God with Us.

And when God with Us walked the dusty roads of Galilee, still he issued the call: "Follow me."

He did not tell those who responded where they were going, or what they would find when they got there. He appealed to the nameless longing, the aching wonder instilled in the human heart from the moment of Creation. He said, *Come out; there is much you have not seen.*

CUT OUT OF THE HERD

Some months ago I attended a Scottish festival held on the campus of a local college. There, during a sheepdog demonstration, I watched a female Border collie, commanded only by silent hand movements from the shepherd, cut out a single ewe from a flock of twenty milling, frightened sheep. With unerring accuracy, the dog zeroed in on her target—running, darting, flattening herself against the ground, swinging wide to flank the sheep on the outside. Within minutes, the ewe stood next to the shepherd, and the dog, obviously pleased with herself, lay grinning and panting at the master's feet.

As I watched, I felt the nameless longing swelling up in my heart. Some change was coming to my life; I didn't know what it was, but I sensed it, the way you sense a storm coming before the clouds begin to bank up on the horizon. It was exciting and adventurous, but a little frightening as well. I was the ewe, and for some reason I was about to be cut out of the herd.

Within a month or two, I began to see a pattern developing in the lives of a number of my close friends. One of my prayer partners, a Lutheran pastor who had been a stalwart support to my spiritual life, sensed a new direction in her ministry and began preparing to accept a call to a new parish, several hundred miles away. My other prayer partner, a woman in her late twenties, quit her job to pursue a degree in theology.

Another longtime friend, both a close personal confidante and a professional colleague, started to move toward a job change that might take her far away. And in my own life, I experienced a subtle shift in priorities, a new direction for my work that could shake some of my carefully laid foundations of financial security.

The supports were being removed. I was being cut out of the herd and brought to the feet of the Shepherd. The Voice was calling: *Come out, Penny; there is much you have not seen.*

ADVENTURING

For all of us who sense the longing to be more than we are, the Voice of the Spirit calls us to come out. Sometimes we face external changes—a shift in job responsibilities, a move to a new city, the loss of old friends, the cultivation of new relationships, the emptying of the nest, isolation through death or divorce. Sometimes the changes are internal, spiritual—falling in love, becoming aware of a long-denied emptiness, facing the challenge of singleness, taking the risk to move into a deeper level of spiritual awareness.

But whatever our change points, whatever our preconceptions, the Voice that calls to us beckons us into the realm of the unknown. The way is not always easy, not always joyous, not always full of light; but it is always, always, an adventure.

We can, of course, choose to remain within the security of the garden wall, in that enclosed place where all is safe and familiar and unthreatening. But something in our spirits causes us to hang over the wall, to climb the nearest tree and gaze wistfully into the woods beyond. There the grass is unclipped, the wild roses tangle in unkempt hedges at the edge of the path.

And Someone is out there, urging us to try, to take the risk, to brave the danger, to find ourselves in the presence of the One who calls.

Perhaps you have stayed within your walls for a long, long time, safe within the refuge of easy answers, where you find security but no growth, protection but no passion. Perhaps you are shielded from the pain that life holds, but you find that those same shields barricade you against love as well.

It is not too late.

Whether you are a novice on the journey or a longtime traveler, the call is the same. There are new vistas to behold, new challenges to meet, new levels of trust and love and faith to experience.

You have felt it.

It is not spring fever. It is the need to go beyond religion into reality. It is the nameless longing our loving God has put within your soul—the desire to reach further, to fly higher, to go deeper, to find within yourself spiritual reserves for a lifetime of journeying.

A great adventure awaits you, just beyond the wall.

Come out, Beloved, the Voice whispers. *There is much you have not seen. . . .*

CHAPTER TWO

The Voiceless Fear

Not fare well,
But fare forward, voyagers.
—T. S. ELIOT

 ackie is standing at a crossroads in her
journey of faith. At age thirty, she has gone back to
college, and she hovers on the threshold of discovering
an entirely new identity, a pristine, unexplored self. "I
feel as if I have been asleep all my life," she told me,
"and I'm only now beginning to awaken."

Jackie has fallen in love with learning.

But the romance has its drawbacks. The dream has its
dark side.

In Jackie's case, it's a literal dark dream—a dream in
which she finds herself standing beside a coffinlike box
that holds all her creative potential, all her hopes for the
future. Her hand is on the latch; in the dream, she knows
that she herself has locked the box, and now it is up to

15

her to unlock it. But she is afraid . . . afraid of what she might find inside. She awakens with the realization that she is the one who must take the risk of releasing that potential—or letting it suffocate.

Two nights ago, Jackie sat in my living room and told me about the dream, about the accompanying heart palpitations and shortness of breath—all the characteristic signs of panic attack.

"I don't understand it," she said. "Sometimes I feel . . . well, excited, with a sense of anticipation. But at other times it's absolute panic—I can't breathe, and I feel my heart pumping like thunder."

Her hand trembles on the latch of the box. And she feels like the mythical Pandora—compelled to open it, but fearful of the outcome.

THE PERPETUAL JOURNEY

No matter where we are in our individual journeys of faith, the Voice in our soul continues to call us to move out, to go deeper, to explore further, to widen our horizons—to move, ultimately, into a more intimate relationship with God.

Sometimes we resist that call. Sometimes we fear.

One of the lamentable shortcomings of the organized church is its apparent inability to encourage its people to move on with God. We establish a sheltered, cushioned religious nest, a place of safety, where expectations are clearly outlined and spiritual maturity can be defined by a checklist.

We apply different names to our comfortable dead-end thought patterns that mark the termination of spiritual growth. Depending upon our doctrinal perspectives, we might say that baptism is "all we need"; or we might identify "rebirth," "sanctification," "the gift of the Holy Spirit" or any number of other concepts as the ultimate goal of spiritual experience. But whatever our particular favorite, all such limited perspectives reduce the nature of our relationship with God to mere fire insurance, a one-way ticket to heaven.

Whatever we call it, God calls it death. A rut is a grave with the ends kicked out. We keep growing, or we die.

God's design is that we continue to flourish and change, to mature and redefine ourselves, throughout our earthly life. "Seeing the glory of the Lord . . ." we "are being transformed into the same image from one degree of glory to another; for this comes from the Lord, the Spirit" (2 Corinthians 3:18, NRSV). God intends for those significant points of grace and epiphany in our life to be way stations, stopovers on the journey of faith . . . not permanent lodgings.

Sometimes we think, as Peter did, that we can live on the Mount of Transfiguration, that we can make a dwelling place in the midst of a momentary glory. But Christ points us outward, down into the valley, further on through the paths of shadow and light, along a way that only God can see.

ADVENTURE ANXIETY

The future is unknown to us. But the call of God is clear.

And so, like Jackie, we step out into a new way of life. We make a commitment that we *know* is right. We begin to look inward to discover the true identity given to us by God. We decide, once and for all, to listen to the Voice calling to us from beyond the wall, to take the risk, to leave the safety of our fortress-home and enter into the terrible beauty of the woods beyond.

And then . . . fear sets in.

We may not be aware of it at first. In the initial flush of excitement, we may know only the sense of adventure, the wonder of new directions.

But somewhere along the way, we begin to *think* about what we've done, about the enormous risks we are taking to leave behind the comfortable, familiar limitations of our life. Like Jackie, we begin to feel the panic.

We have probably felt it before, at the significant turning points in our life:

Freshman fright.

Premarital jitters.

New-parent apprehension syndrome.

And, in the case of the spiritual traveler, *adventure anxiety.*

The anxiety that comes with facing the unknown is a voiceless fear, not tied to specific phobias or linked to particular memories of past trauma. And because it has no fixed object, the voiceless fear can be a difficult dragon to face and vanquish.

We know how it is to be afraid of bats or rats or things that go bump in the night. We understand why we awaken in a cold sweat after a nightmare about being audited by the IRS. And when we sit in the darkness choking back a hard knot of anxiety, listening to sirens and waiting for a long overdue loved one, our fear has an *object,* a *reason.* We can comprehend it, grapple with it, and in some cases overcome it.

But when we face the prospect of spiritual adventure, of growing in intimacy with a God who loves us, fear seems an inappropriate, unsuitable response.

Didn't I hear God calling me?

Don't I trust God to take care of me?

Can't I believe that God wants the best for me?

Shouldn't I be delighted about the new directions God has planned for me?

What's wrong with me, anyway?

FUTURE SHOCK

Change can be threatening. It brings stress, a ruffling of the established nest, an uprooting of the way things used to be. Even positive changes—getting married, having a baby, taking on an exciting new job, moving into a dream house—can be frightening. Familiarity, even negative familiarity, creates a comfort zone: If I know what is likely to happen, I can deal with it, even if it's bad. Even if it's boring. Even if it's stifling in its sameness.

God, however, is not in the business of leaving us to our old familiar patterns. The Spirit says:

> Forget the former things; do not dwell on the past.
> See, I am doing a new thing! Now it springs up;
> do you not perceive it? I am making a way in the
> desert and streams in the wasteland . . . to give
> drink to my people, my chosen, the people I formed
> for myself that they may proclaim my praise.
> (Isaiah 43:18-21)

19

God declares a "new thing" for the People of the Promise—springs in the desert, water in the wasteland. It's an exciting, miraculous, thrilling idea.

Until we realize the catch: We have to *be* in the wilderness to see it happen.

God has to get us out of our comfortable, familiar places, into the wilderness—not a literal desert, but a place of solitude with the Lord—in order to offer us the springs of water. Sometimes God has to get us off by ourselves—through personal struggle, life changes, doubts, questions, unforeseen hardship, or disappointment. The times when we feel alone, misunderstood, isolated, confused—those become our wilderness moments, when God can have our undivided attention and draw close to us in love and understanding.

The Bible is full of wilderness experiences that brought people closer to God. Moses received his call to be the deliverer of Israel in the wilderness. God revealed the divine nature to Elijah in the wilderness. After his baptism, Jesus himself was "driven by the Spirit into the wilderness," where he faced down the enemy and found strength and anointing for his mission. And Mary the mother of Christ had her own kind of wilderness: After the angel announced to her that she would bear the Messiah, he left her alone to face the implications of the Annunciation and sort out what kind of changes God's declaration would mean in her life.

The wilderness is usually not a place we choose to go. We prefer the consolation of the known, the warmth and security of the familiar.

But if we want to experience God's "new thing," we

have to be willing to go out into the wilderness, into the fearful unknown. If we want to see streams gushing up in the wasteland and drink from the living spring, we must venture out into the lonely places with God.

We cannot stay in spiritual suburbia if we want to see the miracle in the desert.

The principle is clear. God is calling us out.

Why, then, are we afraid? Why does Jackie feel heart-pounding panic? Why does the voiceless fear rise up within us—the vague foreboding that has no object, the unidentified apprehension of the future?

Because most of us regard the unknown as a threat rather than a hope.

Two Views of Tomorrow

When I was a child, I was taught—both by precept and by example—that the future held unlimited possibilities for me. I could do anything, be anything, as long as I was willing to commit myself to the dream. Thus the future became for me a bright, exciting realm of infinite potential, and I faced the unknown with anticipation and excitement.

But others—perhaps the majority—have been given a very narrow vision of the possibilities held out before them, with many limitations on their options. For them, the unknown future holds Trouble with a capital *T*, the potential not for achievement but for disaster.

Tragically, most of us have not been taught to view the shadowed future as a magical, mystical wonderland of new experiences and unlimited possibilities. Instead, we have lived like Jackie's creative self in her dream-vision:

21

boxed in, latched down, limited, and contained—but safe.
We have been drilled in the lessons of self-protection,
taught to keep our expectations low:

Don't aim too high.
Don't expect too much.
Stay in your place.
Don't rock the boat.
If you think it can't get worse, just wait.
Murphy's Law is a study in optimism. . . .

We are taught—if not directly, then by implication—
that we are fools to let our heart yearn for greater possibilities; that we will only be hurt by longing for
something deeper.

God disagrees. God has put that longing into our heart.

But we fall for the Big Lie anyway.

We hold back; we put limits on ourselves and say,
"This far, and no farther; this high, and no higher; this
deep, and no deeper." We long for more but dare not
believe that more is possible.

Seldom are we encouraged—by parents, society, family, or even the church—to take a bold plunge into the
unknown, to launch out in response to God's call with
joy and abandon. Instead, we are warned about making
wrong choices. We are told to be careful, to play it safe,
to stay in the shallow end.

We feed the voiceless fear and starve our faith—with
a little help from our friends.

Accustomed to a narrow range of options, we have
trouble comprehending the wideness of the possibilities
God offers to us. And so we face the future—the unknown,
hidden path charted by the loving hand of God—with

panic rather than purpose, with anxiety instead of anticipation. The future threatens instead of beckons.

But it does not have to be so.

EMBRACING THE HIDDEN PATH

The unknown, hidden paths of our spiritual journey do not *have* to be a source of fear for us—if our focus is in the right place.

God, it is true, does not tell us what paths are marked out for us. We have no divine road map, no curved mirrors to see around the bend ahead, no way of knowing what tomorrow will hold.

It has always been this way, of course—God's wisdom withholds the future from us, for our own good. We are creatures who crave control; we want to see everything, analyze everything, and choose the logical direction, the shortest distance to our destination.

These patterns are established early in life, as anyone knows who has traveled great distances in a car with small children: "When are we gonna be there, Daddy? Why are we going this way? The sun is in my eyes! I need to go to the bathroom . . . I'm hungry . . . I'm thirsty . . . I'm tired. Mommy, Jason touched me! I don't want to ride in the car anymore. ARE WE THERE YET?"

Sometimes our dialogue with God on the spiritual journey holds faint echoes of those wonderful family vacations. We want to know: *Where are we going? Why are we going this way? Are we there yet?*

But God's priorities are different from our own. To the Lord, our journey is not a breakneck race toward a fixed destination—that elusive goal called *spiritual maturity*—

but an opportunity for a long drive in the country. If we wish to have joy in the journey, we need to realize one all-important truth: God is concerned with the *process*. It is important that we walk with Someone; where we go on the journey does not always lie within our control.

Once we take the risk to come out from the safety of the walled garden, we will most certainly face the voiceless fear of the great unknown. For we cannot, in any ultimate sense, see where we are going.

But we do know the God who goes with us — the God who loves us, the God who promises:

> I will lead the blind by ways they have not known, along unfamiliar paths I will guide them; I will turn the darkness into light before them and make the rough places smooth. These are the things I will do; I will not forsake them. (Isaiah 42:16)

Sometimes the way is dark.

Sometimes the path seems to disappear.

Sometimes, like Jackie, you panic and hear nothing but your heart's pulse roaring in your ears.

But the Voice that called you out is near, still calling: *Come out; there is much you have not seen.*

And when the future seems uncertain, and your memories are crowded with the voices of the multitude crying, "Turn back! Turn back before it's too late," then remember . . .

You are not alone.

The One who walks beside you knows the woods beyond the wall.

CHAPTER THREE

The Unseen Danger

Go, go, go, said the bird: human kind
Cannot bear very much reality.
   —T. S. ELIOT

Matt had listened to the Voice calling to him from beyond the garden wall. He believed that God was directing him to make some radical changes in his life. The new teaching position he had been offered held some wonderful opportunities: to communicate his faith to his students, to grow in his own spiritual life, to make a difference—a real difference—in the lives of others.

And so Matt uprooted his wife and children and moved them halfway across the country, away from family and friends and familiar surroundings. He took a salary reduction and left his unsold house in the hands of a trusted real estate agent.

At first it was a wonderful adventure. Matt plunged into teaching with a zeal born of the knowledge that he was right where the Lord wanted him. His students loved him; his classes were always full. He really *was* making a difference. And his heart overflowed with gratitude to the God who had led him.

Then, a few months into the new job, reality kicked in. Things began to go wrong. Matt's wife was unhappy and lonely. The children weren't adjusting well to their new school. The house back East hadn't sold, and double payments were eating away at their savings. It looked as if Matt's only option was to let the house go into foreclosure and declare personal bankruptcy.

Matt prayed. All his friends prayed. He had trusted God with his life, his family, his future. He had been obedient. So why were things so terribly, terribly hard?

LIVING HAPPILY EVER AFTER?

In the first flush of falling in love, it's easy to believe that my beloved can do no wrong, that all our struggles will be little ones, that we will indeed live happily ever after.

We call it a "fairy-tale romance." The Dream Job. The Perfect Life. But upon closer inspection, even the fairy tales we grew up with offer no such easy answers. Oh, things turn out well enough in the end. But not before Hansel and Gretel have their innocent little lives threatened; not before Cinderella suffers abuse at the hands of her evil stepsisters; not before Snow White is poisoned by the wicked stepmother.

In every fairy tale, we always find an element of danger, a wicked witch or an evil sorcerer who sets out to kill the good little boys and girls.

Fairy tales give us a surprisingly accurate picture of real life. But we usually don't think about them that way. We'd rather focus on the happy ending and forget about the life-threatening circumstances that precede the final resolution.

The principle carries over into our spiritual life as well. We fall in love with Jesus and expect the relationship to be lifelong bliss, uninterrupted happiness and fulfillment. We take the first step on a new spiritual adventure; we answer the call to come out from the safety of the walled garden. And then we are surprised—dismayed, even—to find that the forest which looked so peaceful holds hidden threats and dangers, wild beasts and shrouded pathways.

It's time to face reality.

If we intend to make the journey, we need to count the cost of following the Voice that has called us forth.

There Be Dragons Here

In ancient times, when men and women held to the certainty that the world was flat, maps of the seas often depicted the end of the earth as a huge cliff. There, a cataract of ocean waters plunged forever into a bottomless chasm, and near the edge of the waterfall, the charts bore the warning: *There Be Dragons Here.*

Sometimes I think I should write that warning, or a modified version of it, on the face page of my Bible.

The reality of the dragons, of the struggles we must face if we leave the protection of our safe places, in no way contradicts the promises of a loving God. But we need to be very clear about the promises. God does not promise happiness; God offers growth. The Lord holds out challenge, not comfort; fortitude, not escape. God's primary goal for us is that we be "conformed to the likeness of his Son" (Romans 8:29).

The Son who learned obedience through suffering.

The Son who sweat blood as he prayed that he might be spared the final agony that awaited him.

The Son who was betrayed by the kiss of a friend.

The Son who let himself be crucified, and cried out with his final breath, "My God, why have you forsaken me?"

You and I are all too familiar with those struggles. You have known suffering, unanswered prayer, betrayal, forsakenness. So have I. But when we take the ultimate risk and pray, "Lord God, make me like Jesus," we don't always want to face the hard truth—to admit that our suffering, our aloneness, our pain, may turn out to be important elements in the process of that transformation.

Theoretically, we know that God uses every experience of our life to accomplish the divine purpose in us. But still we resist. We try to persuade the Lord that an easy life would do the job as well as a difficult one.

So far, God doesn't seem convinced.

So, as we set foot on the path, striking out on the glorious adventure of spiritual journeying, we need to remember that things are not always what they seem. The validity of God's call does not negate the inherent dangers of the forest.

St. Cyril of Jerusalem wrote:

> The dragon sits by the side of the road, watching those who pass. Beware lest he devour you. We go

to the Father of Souls, but it is necessary to pass by the dragon.*

When the Shaper of Souls calls us out, his Voice summons us to risk, to venture forth, to trust. If there be dragons here, the Lord has called us to face them as well.

But we don't want to face them.

We don't even want to acknowledge the possibility of dragons along our path.

We want things to be easy, comfortable, secure.

And yet that nameless longing remains, urging us to take the risk, to step out, to let the Voice lead us to an unknown land.

We can't have it both ways.

We have to decide—here, now, with the Voice whispering in our ears, *Come out; there is much you have not seen.*

And precisely because we have not seen it, because we do not know what dangers await us, because we cannot anticipate what may happen, the decision to follow must be a leap of faith. We must trust—not in our own understanding, or in our own ability to handle whatever dangers lie ahead, but in the trustworthiness of the One who calls us.

Only God knows what lies beyond the raging waterspout at the edge of the world.

GETTING THE LARGER VIEW

When Adam and Eve ate from the Tree of the Knowledge of Good and Evil and were barred from Paradise, they were sent into a wilderness where thorns

---

*Quoted in Flannery O'Connor, *Mystery and Manners* (New York: Farrar, Straus, & Giroux, 1957), 35.

grew more abundantly than fruit, where pain and blood-shed accompanied reproduction. We read about "the curse" of sweat and tears and labor and blood, and sometimes God seems like a hard taskmaster.

But the Bible indicates that the Lord's decision to banish them from the Garden was, at least in part, for their own benefit: "[They] must not be allowed to reach out . . . and take also from the tree of life and eat, and live forever" (Genesis 3:22).

As we read these words and sense the anguish of our first parents at the loss of Paradise, we must remember the Lord's perspective, the Almighty's long-range inten-tion for the children of God's heart. The expulsion from the Garden of Eden was as much a protection as a punish-ment. God did not want them to live forever . . . *in sin.*

Already, before the foundations of the earth were ever laid, God had made provision for the redemption of humankind. God was able, as they were not, to look down the long vistas of history and see another tree, standing on a barren hill, a tree whose fruit promised eternal life to all who acknowledged their sin and received the sacrifice of body and blood.

When God created Adam and Eve, even before calling them out of the garden and into the wilderness, the Lord put within them—and within us—that nameless longing, the desire for something better, something deeper; the vague sense that somehow we are called to be more than we are. Distorted, that desire ended in sin and brought death and destruction into the world.

And yet the Lord did not see fit to obliterate the long-ing. Instead, the Spirit pointed them—and us—beyond

the desert places, to the Cross . . . and beyond the
Cross, to other desert places, difficult journeys, joys
and sorrows, battles and triumphs. God pointed to the
process, the long journey that would transform us and
make us all we were created to be as sons and daughters
of God.

Tragically, we have made that longing, that sense of
call, into an end in itself rather than the first step of a
journey toward discovery. We have made the Cross the
culmination rather than the beginning of our spiritual
pilgrimage.

"Come to Jesus," we say, either directly or implicitly,
"and your dreams will be realized, your problems
solved." We speak of victories, but ignore the violent
battles that precede them. We talk of new birth, but
prefer not to think of the pain and tears and blood
and agony that accompany labor. We glory in the
Resurrection, but romanticize the Crucifixion until the
grisly torture of that execution is excised and all that
remains is a peaceful, loving, forgiving Christ smiling
down upon us.

But the glory, the victory, the resurrection, is not the
whole story. Coming to Jesus is not enough—any more
than being born is enough. We have to grow up sometime.

LEAVING NEVER NEVER LAND

When I was a child, I saw the classic Disney movie
Peter Pan. Like every other child in the theater, I was
entranced with Tinker Bell and the possibility of flying,
and I shouted as loud as anyone, "I believe!" when Tink
was dying. But one element of the plot puzzled me: I

didn't understand for the life of me why anyone would want to live in Never Never Land, the place where you never grow up.

I *wanted* to grow up—partly, I suppose, to be free from my parents, who (like all parents) always seemed to be telling me what to do. But even more, I longed for that magical time when I would make my own decisions, be my own person, live in my own house, keep my own hours. I wanted to be *mature*.

I never, never wanted to live in Never Never Land.

Now I live in my own house, make my own decisions, keep my own hours. I also pay my own mortgage, cook my own meals, and wash my own clothes. I've given up some of the freedoms of youth and taken on some of the responsibilities of adulthood.

It's a trade-off.

The spiritual life, too, is a kind of trade-off. When we follow the Voice that calls us out, we lose the security of the familiar, the walled garden where nothing can harm us. We face the unseen dangers, the dragons lurking by the side of the road.

Sometimes we get hurt.

Sometimes we become afraid and question whether we've made the right choice in the first place.

But sometimes we overcome the dragons.

And then we look around us at the beauty and delight of the woods beyond the wall and wonder why we waited so long to step out.

There be dragons here. There be dangers, and struggles. Like every other change in life, it's a trade-off.

But it's worth it.

THE DREAM FULFILLED

Joseph, the dreamer, heard the Voice of God calling him out, setting him apart.* He saw, in his youthful dreams, the Lord's promise to make him a ruler over many people. But the fulfillment of that promise was a long time coming, and the beginning stages of that fulfillment hardly looked like the work of a loving God.

Joseph's brothers, angry over his arrogant attitude and jealous of his father's favoritism, sold him into slavery. Joseph ended up as a servant in the house of a high Egyptian official named Potiphar. When he refused the advances of Potiphar's wife, she falsely accused him of rape, and her accusation landed him in prison.

It took thirteen years before Joseph began to see the fulfillment of his dreams.

Or did it?

Is it possible—even imaginable—that the fulfillment of Joseph's call began the moment his brothers sold him to the caravan of slave traders headed for Egypt?

If we believe that God is interested in the *process* as well as the *outcome* of our life, we get our first glimpse of the value of the difficulties and struggles we must face. Joseph's dreams were not postponed in those years between seventeen and thirty, when he endured slavery and imprisonment and false accusation and betrayal. His character was being formed.

God had to make Joseph a ruler on the inside before he could stand next to Pharaoh and take his place as second in command in the land of Egypt.

Joseph's experience was not a postponement of the

*The story of Joseph is told in Genesis 37 and 39–50.

dream. It was part of the realization. God didn't *cause* Joseph's suffering, but God did *use* it to bring Joseph into the reality of his calling.

We've heard it before—how suffering instills nobility, how struggles make us strong. And sometimes we get tired of all this talk about character building. We don't like the idea that the peaceful-looking forest beyond the garden wall may hold hidden dangers. We don't want to believe that *There Be Dragons Here.* And we certainly don't want to admit that God may be calling us forth for the very purpose of facing them.

A friend of mine once joked, "If suffering deepens your character, maybe I'll just stay shallow. . . ."

It sounds like an attractive alternative. But is it, really?

No Longer an Option

Recently I sent a card to a close friend who is going through major changes and uncertainties in her life. On the front of the card, a young woman stood at the crossroad of a path through the woods. One arm of the directional sign, pointing into the woods, said, YOUR LIFE. The other, pointing back the way she had come, said, NO LONGER AN OPTION.

Technically, of course, we do have the option to "just stay shallow." We can accept without question. We can stifle our doubts and fears; we can keep up the pretense that we experience the "victorious Christian life" on a daily basis. We can say all the right words and make sure our behavior conforms to the accepted norms. We can repeat the pat answers. We can maintain the charade.

It's possible to keep up the front. I've done it—I did it for years. Perhaps you've done it as well. It's draining; it's exhausting; it's depressing . . . but it is possible. And it does keep you protected from those nagging, insidious questions about reality.

But if you have heard the Voice calling from beyond the garden wall, if you have felt the nameless longing, if you have abandoned the safety of the garden to enter the dark woods, the pretense is too heavy a burden to bear. Turning back is *no longer an option.*

For your heart is now opened to something deeper, something more real, something truer than you have ever known.

It's a risk, all right.

When the first dark night comes, you probably will wonder if you have made the right decision. You may long to go back to the safety of your walls, to the security of the familiar. You may sense the presence of an unseen danger and feel the stab of fear.

You may even doubt everything that you have been taught before.

But you have taken the first step on a journey of discovery: discovery of yourself, and of God.

Trust.

Trust God to sift out the reality as wheat is garnered from chaff.

Trust God to forge, through whatever difficulties you face, a person of strength and integrity and fidelity.

There are unseen dangers in the woods beyond the wall. There be dragons here.

But there are also unfamiliar joys and passions, unknown freedoms, unexpected fulfillments.

The spiritual journey into reality offers only one guarantee: In the long run, you will gain more than you lose.

Trust.

God knows what lies beyond the edges of your world.

TWO

Into the Beckoning Woods

She must have slept. The moon had risen, but its light brought little comfort. The pale reflection threw phantoms of movement into the darkness around her. Gnarled branches transformed into hands reaching out to grab her; shifting leaves made every root at her feet jump into serpentine life. She held her breath and shrank into the tree trunk at her back.

Then she heard, once more, the Voice. *Quester?* it called softly. Was she dreaming? She pinched her arm until it hurt, then listened again. *Come out, Quester; there is much you have not seen.*

"Who's there?" Her reply was little more than a

squeaky whisper. She gulped the damp forest air into her lungs and called again, "Who's there?"

It is I, Quester. Come out; there is much you have not seen.

She recognized the Voice; without a doubt, it was the one who had called to her — not once, but many times, in many dreams. And always the Voice said the same words, urging her on in low tones, gently persistent. In the dreams she had assumed the Voice trustworthy, benevolent. Her heart had responded instinctively, as much to the alluring sound as to the words themselves.

Now Quester did not know if the Voice could be trusted. The woods had transformed in the darkness; perhaps the one who called to her intended merely to lure her from the safety of her home into an unfriendly world where, as her mother had warned her, dangers awaited.

She peered into the shadows before her. Clouds banked against the moon, plunging Quester and the woods around her into a sudden blackness. She gasped and threw her hands out before her, caught by the smothering claustrophobia brought on by utter dark. The night became a living, breathing entity, wrapping itself around her. She could feel it closing in.

Then she felt something else. A hand, half again as large as her own, closed around her fingers. It lifted her to her feet, drawing her close to a presence she could not see—a thrilling, dangerous, overwhelming presence.

"I am Guardian," the Voice said softly. "Will you come with me? There is much you have not seen."

"I can see nothing now," Quester said, a bit startled by her own boldness. "You are the one who has called me out?"

"Yes," he replied. "I spoke to you in dreams, and put the longing in your heart to walk through the gate and into these woods. Will you come with me?"

"Where are we going?"

"In time, you shall see. Or perhaps not."

"You are speaking riddles!" The fear in Quester's heart leaped into words. "Will you not tell me where you are taking me?"

"Perhaps the question is, 'Where are *you* taking *me?*'" Quester felt rather than saw a glimmer of a smile. Was he making fun of her? The invisible hand squeezed hers gently, and he said, "If we merely walk together, we shall come to the place we need to be."

She was not satisfied. "Do I have to go?"

"Dear Child, of course not!" A deep chuckle rumbled above Quester's head, in the vicinity where she assumed his chest would be. "You are quite free to choose what you shall do. You may come with me, for there is much you have not seen, or you may return to the safety of your home. The garden gate stands open for your return. You may go back—if you can."

"If I can find my way back, you mean?"

"No, Child." He laughed softly once more. "You can certainly find your way back. But can you accept going back the way you came?"

Quester thought she was beginning to understand. If she refused to go now to see what she had not seen, could she return and live in a walled garden for the rest of her days?

She sighed heavily and resolutely took a step in the direction of the Voice. "Yes, I will go. I can always come back if I want to."

Guardian took her hand again and began to lead her away, striding through the dark woods. "Perhaps," the Voice murmured. "Perhaps."

CHAPTER FOUR

The Terrible Risk of Birth

The Word in the desert
Is most attacked by voices of temptation.
  —T. S. ELIOT

Last night, for the third time, I watched
Steel Magnolias — a touching movie filled with humor
and pathos, spiritual insight, human struggle, and the
triumph of love over pain. In that film Shelby, a young
woman in her twenties, is ravaged by severe diabetes
and warned that pregnancy could threaten her life.
When she announces to her mother that she is expecting, the mother is angry and refuses to rejoice with her,
too concerned over her daughter's health to consider
anything else.

"You always said you just wanted me to be happy,"
Shelby says as she confronts her mother about her
attitudes. "Well, I'd rather have thirty minutes of wonderful than a lifetime of nothing special."

Shelby understood the risk of birth.

All my life I have heard that when a woman gives birth, she forgets the pain as soon as she experiences the joy of holding that squirming, wrinkled, bawling infant in her arms. But one friend recently said to me, "Don't believe it. My daughter is twenty-five, and I still remember every bit of the pain. I'd do it again, in a minute, but I do remember . . . there is nothing romantic about childbirth."

In spiritual terms, too, there is nothing innately "romantic" about giving birth to new life. Conception is risky business; delivery is agonizing. A child, a book, a new idea, a different life direction, a new spiritual adventure, a soul . . . always, birth is a difficult, painful, bloody process.

It is worth it, of course. Once we get through it and look back on the experience from the other side, we often feel that we'd "do it again, in a minute." But while we are in the throes of labor, while the pain is coming hard and fast, we dare not romanticize the risk of birth.

You Must Be Born Again

Early in Jesus' ministry, shortly after his first miracle of turning water into wine at the wedding feast in Cana, he was approached—by night, in the darkness— by a leader of the Jews, a Pharisee named Nicodemus (John 3:1-10).

To this pillar of the community, this religious man who kept all the laws fastidiously and presented himself as a spiritual example, Jesus said, "You must be born again."

You must be born again . . . you must enter into new life, take the risk of birth, launch out, and follow the Voice that is calling you from the safety of your walled garden.

Nicodemus didn't quite understand. He took Jesus' words too literally: "How can anyone be born after having grown old?" he asked. "Can one enter a second time into the mother's womb and be born?" (NRSV).

The Pharisee's argument is a logical one: *I am an adult — too old, too big, too set in my ways to be reborn now. How can I go back and start over after all these years?*

And Jesus says, "You must be born again."

In a way, Nicodemus was right. Being born is a one-way tunnel into life; we can't go back again, can't reenter the womb and try for a second chance. If we could, we might be tempted to stay in the womb forever . . . in that safe, protected place where all our needs are met and we don't have to face the harsh light of reality.

But Jesus, of course, was speaking of a different kind of birth . . . a renewal of the soul, nurtured in the womb of the Spirit, a divine calling-out into a place of growth and change and maturing into the image of the One who created us. Once we leave the sheltered environment of our spiritual infancy, we outgrow it. We don't fit anymore.

We can't go back again.

But we can go forward.

BORN INTO THE LIGHT

It's a frightening concept, new birth . . . to be catapulted like helpless infants into an unfamiliar, perhaps hostile world . . . to give ourselves over, heart and soul, to the God who calls us out into new life, into new experiences, into deep spiritual waters.

And rebirth is not simply a matter of a once-and-for-all point of epiphany that will carry us to the grave. Many of us, of course, have a single identifiable moment of confrontation with the Almighty . . . an experience we identify as our initial point of "new birth." We make a deliberate decision to respond to the grace of God and embrace the Lord's purposes in our life.

I have such a marking point in my own spiritual journey—September 15, 1970, the night I awakened to a conscious awareness that God's Spirit was grappling with my heart. Like Jacob struggling in pitched battle with the angel, I had the choice to surrender, or to continue resisting.

I surrendered. It was a moment of rebirth for me.

But when I look back upon my spiritual history and see the successes and failures of my life with God—the times of obedience and joy, the times of rebellion and heartache—I see that there were other moments of epiphany as well. Both before and after my experience of surrender on September 15, 1970, I can see the hand of God working in my life, drawing me toward spiritual consciousness, leading me on the journey of faith, even when I was unaware of being on the path.

And all along the way, I see altars of sacrifice, times in which God called me to a new place, a different level of intimacy, continued growth.

As important as that one significant moment can be, we must not stop there. We must take the risk to go forward as God leads us to new levels of life in the Spirit.

But sometimes we get stuck. Like Nicodemus, we fall prey to the temptation to rest on our reputations, to allow others to perceive us as pillars of righteousness and examples of faith, when we have, somewhere along the line, stopped growing. We become spiritually atrophied, set in our ways, unwilling to launch out and take risks. Comfortable and complacent, we are satisfied with the status quo.

Then Jesus comes to us with the disturbing word: "You must be born again."

"But, Lord," the argument begins, "I've already been born . . . remember, fifteen years ago when I committed my life to you? Why, I've been ministering in your name for years! Look how many people I've influenced; look at all I've done. . . ."

Call it what you will: rebirth, recommitment, resurrection, awakening . . . God calls it risking everything for the sake of the new life that lies beckoning us onward.

MIRACLE AMID CHAOS

"I feel as if I've come into a whole new life," a close friend of mine told me recently. "As if I've been reborn all over again."

I listened while she shared her story: God had been working in her life over a period of many months, bringing her to the point of dealing with some extremely difficult issues of abuse in her past that resulted in immeasurable pain and struggle in the present. For a long time she had been more or less comfortable with her life, unaware of the raging turmoil of anguish that festered below the surface of consciousness.

Now God was bringing those dark things to light and, in the process of healing, showing them to her one by one. The journey toward facing reality was sheer agony, and as she grappled with the truth, many of the formerly stable props of her carefully constructed life were giving way.

Still, she rejoiced in finding out the truth—about herself, about her relationships, about her past . . . and, in the long run, about God's directions for her in the future.

"In the midst of all the chaos," she said, "I'm finding my faith again—faith not in other people, who have betrayed me or denied my pain; but in God alone . . . in a God who adores me and looks lovingly upon me, a God who sees me as a person of infinite worth."

The miracle always comes to us in the midst of chaos—or brings chaos in its wake.* When the blind man in John 9 received his sight at the hands of the Messiah, he wasn't fully aware of what was happening to him. He only knew that he had mud on his face, and so he went and washed.

He washed. And his entire life was turned upside down: He lost his job—he couldn't beg for a living because he was no longer blind. He lost the support of his family—they were afraid of the Pharisees' reaction. He even lost his right to worship—he was cast out of the synagogue, driven from fellowship.

He might have refused the miracle. At least when he was blind, he had a job. At least when he was blind, he had the support of his friends and family. At least when he was blind, he had fellowship.

Once his miracle was accomplished, he was left

*For the generation of these ideas about miracle and chaos, I am indebted to a sermon preached by Pastor John Thorstensen, Grace Lutheran Church, Fairmont, Minnesota.

with nothing. Nothing but Jesus, who came to him in his isolation. Nothing but a new life. Nothing but his sight.

THE WONDERFUL, TERRIBLE RISK

When we answer the call of God, the Voice from beyond the garden wall urging us to come out, we take a terrible, wonderful risk. If we respond to the miracle of epiphany, the astonishing spectacle of sight, we risk leaving behind all we have known before, everything that has brought us security and comfort.

We can, like Nicodemus, make excuses: *I'm too old to be born . . . I cannot enter into the womb again and start over.* Or we can choose, like the blind man, to embrace the miracle with all its chaos, leave behind our dependence upon others, and walk into the light.

The light may, at first, seem blinding.

The chaos may seem unnecessary, and unfair.

But once we take the risk of birth, the shell of our former life falls away to reveal a new world, a world of wonder and growth, a world of awe and mystery. Once we wash away the mud, we find that our eyes, miraculously, have been opened.

And we see Jesus there.

The Voice that calls us from the safety of our walled gardens offers us no promises of an easy way or ready answers. Guardian holds out no guarantees of protection from chaos or from the pain of birth.

We only know that the Voice has called, and that wherever we go, the One who loves us will go with us.

CHAPTER FIVE

Hard Questions

In order to arrive at what you do not know,
You must go by a way which is the way of ignorance.
—T. S. ELIOT

I'm planning a trip for Memorial Day weekend. I've got all the maps out, and I've charted my route with a yellow marker. I know where the highways run, and how long it should take me to reach my destination. I've made careful plans.

But I don't know how heavy the traffic will be, where the stretches of road construction might slow down my progress . . . or what I will find when I get there. I have reservations at a resort described in the travel brochures, a room with a view overlooking a lake. The photos in the advertisements are beautiful. I hope for the best. I pray it won't rain. But until I arrive . . . well, I won't really know.

Human experience is full of such questions and

uncertainties, some more significant than others. It's not a matter of life and death, after all, whether or not the resort I've chosen *really* looks like it does in the pictures. But other questions—questions about God's direction for my future, how the decisions I make now will affect me five years from now—cause me greater anxiety.

I want to *know*. I want *answers*.

When God calls us out from the safety of our walled gardens and challenges us to walk into the unknown forest, we sometimes mistakenly assume that, just because we are being led, all those hard questions will be answered. I've taken this risk, after all. I've been obedient. I've responded. Doesn't God owe me some assurances in return?

The truth is, when we accept the invitation to go deeper with God, we may find that our decision raises more questions than it answers.

The forest is not quite what we imagined in our dreams. Far from being a beautiful, safe place of peace and pastoral delights, it may appear as a foreboding, even dangerous wilderness. Our Guardian is there with us, yes, but that doesn't mean that all our fears and doubts are instantly resolved. Now we have more questions than ever . . . beginning with the basic question: "Have I really made the right choice?"

If I take this step of faith—if I commit myself in marriage, purchase this house, enter counseling to deal with problem areas in my life, accept a new job with greater risk and greater potential—what will happen? What will be the results? Will it work? Is it *right?*

As much as we may long to know and do the will of

God, we cannot always be sure of the outcome of the decisions we make. The Lord does not always tell us what will happen if we obey God's will. Sometimes God does not even tell us what that will is.

The path of faith is sometimes the way of ignorance.

Walking the Way of Unknowing

I recently had a conversation with a young friend—Joy, a little girl of eight who was facing changes in her family life and was a bit anxious about the outcome.

"Penny," she asked in a quiet, apprehensive voice, "if all this stuff changes—if we move, and everything's different—well, what's going to happen? What's it going to be like?"

I thought for a few minutes, and then I said, "Sweetie, I honestly don't know."

I was a little afraid that Joy might be upset at my inability to give her the kind of reassurances she needed. But then she began to giggle. "You're the first grown-up I've ever known who told me, 'I don't know,'" she said. "Usually they make something up, whether they know or not."

She's right, I thought. *Usually we make something up so that we don't have to admit that we don't know everything.*

Historically, the church has had a difficult time admitting to the inherent ignorance of the human mind. We think we're *supposed* to know, to have all the answers—not just for ourselves, but for everyone else as well. We latch on to a Bible verse such as "We have the mind of Christ" (1 Corinthians 2:16) and play those words to ourselves like a magical incantation until, forgetting our human limitations, we begin to believe that we can comprehend the infinite mind of God.

"Jesus is the answer," we proclaim. And the world's cynical bumper-sticker reply is, "So what's the question?"

It's an appropriate response.

There are no easy answers. If we're honest, we know that there aren't even any easy questions. Sometimes we don't know what to ask. Sometimes God doesn't give us much to go on.

But we don't like living with uncertainty. We prefer checklists, black-and-white absolutes, a pattern, an updated map to follow that will get us to our destination in the shortest possible time with the least amount of hardship. And we're much more comfortable if everyone around us accepts our checklists as well.

And so we establish universal responses that are supposed to apply generically to all situations:

- If your marriage is in trouble, go to a Marriage Encounter weekend and—presto!—put the romance back in your life.
- If your kid is on drugs, pray.
- If you're angry with someone, forgive.
- If you struggle with sin patterns, confess and repent.
- If you have a difficult decision to make, ask God for the answer and watch for the signs. Put out a fleece. Wait for the dew to fall.

But what if the dew doesn't fall? What if you're in a drought that has gone on for years? What if no answers come? What if life just doesn't seem to make any sense?

Or, heaven forbid, what if you have to decide between two *good* possibilities?

THE MYSTERY TRIP

If we truly want to walk with God, to reach out beyond our comfort zones and take the risk to go deeper, we need to set aside our compulsive desire for answers.

Jesus, after all, did not say, "I am the answer." He said, "I am the way" (John 14:6).

Distinguishing between the *way* and the *answer* is essentially an issue of perception. The road map is an *answer*. The beckoning path into the recesses of the forest is a *way*.

My friend Helen used to take me on what she called "mystery trips." She would declare a day to be set aside, and then tell me no more. When the day came, we would get in the car and drive to . . . well, to wherever she was taking me. And she didn't put up with any nonsense. When I began to ask, "Where are we going? What are we going to do?" she would simply grin at me and reply, "Don't ask any questions."

Once she took me to a thoroughbred pig race; once to a concert; once to a threshing festival. I never knew. I had to trust her . . . trust her to know where we were going, trust her to make the plans. She gave me no answers at all; she simply led the way.

The spiritual journey often seems like an extended "mystery trip." God does not tell us, "Don't ask any questions," but even as we ask, we need to be prepared to accept the fact that sometimes God withholds the answers. We may not be ready to know. Or we may need the experience of trusting God even when we don't understand.

The Bible gives ample evidence of God's ability to be trusted in the midst of unanswered questions. Moses asked *who*. Who was this God who called to him to come out from the people of Egypt and lead a nation of slaves into freedom? And God responded with the cryptic answer, "I am Who I am" (Exodus 3:14).

Job asked *why*. Why, if Job was truly righteous in God's sight, did the Lord take everything from him? Job's friends tried to answer the question for him and failed. Then God answered, not by telling Job *why* in specific terms, but by opening Job's eyes to the Divine Mystery. And for Job, that was enough. He responded, "My ears had heard of you but now my eyes have seen you. Therefore I . . . repent" (Job 42:5-6).

Abraham asked *where*. Where was the Lord leading him? What was his final destination? And God told him only, "Leave your country, your people and your father's household and go to the land I will show you" (Genesis 12:1).

Gideon asked *how*. He was not a "mighty warrior," as the Lord referred to him. How could he, an ordinary, humble man, be used of God to save Israel from the Midianites? God answered him not with a battle plan, but with an assurance of the Lord's presence: "I will be with you." (Judges 6:16).

Even the strong, "mighty warriors," the biblical giants of our faith-heritage, the men and women we look to as models of trust, were flawed, insecure, questioning people.

And so are we. We bombard the Lord — or ourselves —
with a barrage of questions about the future, about our
destination, about God's plan. And often the answer we
receive is the same:

> *I will be with you.*
> *I will show you.*
> *I am Who I am.*

God is with us. It is enough.

LEAPING INTO THE GAP

In the action-packed movie *Indiana Jones and the
Last Crusade,* Indiana's quest is to find the Holy Grail,
the chalice used by Christ at the Last Supper. But to
reach the Grail, Indy must face life-threatening
challenges that test his humility, his obedience, and
his trust.

In the final challenge, Indiana finds himself teetering
on one side of a deep, vast chasm. The way across,
according to the legends, lies right before him, but he cannot see it. He must step out in faith, with no tangible
assurance of support. He must leap into the gap. He must
trust what his eyes cannot discern.

Fearful but determined, Indy steps out . . . and discov-
ers himself standing on a bridge of rock, solid and firm
beneath his feet but invisible to the eye. He still must
walk the bridge; he still must call upon his faith and
discernment to retrieve the Grail, but the way is open
before him.

Sometimes in our attempts to follow God's will, we,

too, may face invisible bridges. We are called to trust, to reach out beyond our knowledge and understanding, to commit ourselves to a journey we do not control and cannot always comprehend.

As we walk with God into the unknown future, we, too, must trust the foundation, the solid, invisible bridge that stretches out before us. We do not always know the destination. We may not see the path, but the One who leads us knows the way.

The One who called us, our Guardian and Guide, waits for us with an outstretched hand, urging us to walk forward into the unknown, into the forest, beyond anything we have experienced or imagined.

In *Prince Caspian,* the second book of C. S. Lewis's Chronicles of Narnia, the children get hopelessly lost trying to find Caspian. The great lion Aslan appears to the child Lucy in the middle of the night and beckons her to follow him. She rouses her brothers and sister, but they are resistant because they don't see the lion. They have only Lucy's word for the fact that he is there at all.

After much debate and hostility, the children waste a great deal of time going around in circles, refusing to follow Lucy's lead. She gives in and goes with them. A few nights later, Aslan finally appears to Lucy again. Ashamed of her disobedience, she asks Aslan what *would have happened* if she had left the others and followed him alone. And he responds:

> "To know what *would* have happened, child?" said
> Aslan. "No. Nobody is ever told that. . . . But any-

one can find out what *will* happen. . . . There is only one way of finding out."*

You can never know what *would have happened* if you had made your decisions differently. But you can find out what *will* happen . . . by responding to the call and taking the risk to step out and follow.

There is much you have not seen. There are many questions that have no answers, many dilemmas that have no solution.

But there is only one way to find out.

Go forward . . . into the risk, into the darkness, into the unknown.

Trust.

Believe.

Act.

Set aside the *answer* and embrace the *way.*

Take the hand of the One who leads you, and walk on.

---

*C. S. Lewis, *Prince Caspian* (New York: Macmillan Publishing Co., 1967), 137.

CHAPTER SIX

You Can't Go Home Again

The only wisdom we can hope to acquire
Is the wisdom of humility: humility is endless.
—T. S. ELIOT

I don't understand it; every time I go home, I shrink."

James was forty-two, a successful man, well-established in his own business. The consummate professional, he nevertheless dreaded his occasional trips home to visit his parents.

"When I drive into town, I begin to feel it happening," he said. "I'm no longer an adult; I become a child. I argue with my parents about the same old issues—issues that should have been resolved years ago. They have expectations of me that I can't meet, and they treat me like they did when I was ten."

He paused and sighed. "But I guess I have to admit that in some ways, I like it . . . just a little. I like having Mom do my laundry and cook my meals. I enjoy being free from the pressures of adult life for just a little while. And I hate myself for liking it."

Occasionally, all of us long to "go home again." We may chafe against the uncomfortable "shrinking" that inevitably happens when we enter our parents' homes, and we may resist their subconscious attempts to treat us like the children we once were. But on another level, we enjoy retreating to a place where we don't have to take responsibility for ourselves, where someone else cares for our needs and relieves us of the duties of ordering our own life.

Some people, however, try to "go home" in a literal, more permanent sense. The financial and social pressures of life in the nineties have forced thousands of adult children to take up residence with their parents. For some, this is a temporary measure so that they can further their education or save for a home of their own—a stopgap on the way to independence. But some simply don't want to face the harsh realities of the "real world." They let Mom and Dad take care of the necessities of life and never learn to stand on their own.

And others opt for a subtler kind of retreat from reality. A woman may move from the sheltering protection of Daddy and take up with Hubby, still playing the childhood princess role, insisting that the man in her life cater to her every whim. Men sometimes play at Peter Pan, living like little boys, expecting in their wives the nurturing Mama who will provide for all their needs.

We may shake our heads in dismay at such childish lack of responsibility. But in spiritual terms, Christians are often enticed by an even more insidious snare: the temptation to remain as spiritual babes, being spoon-fed the pabulum of someone else's faith. We shrink from the responsibility of caring for our own spiritual needs; we prefer the safety of the walled garden. And when God calls us out into the realm of the unknown, we are terrified of the risk and want to make sure that we have a safety net — the possibility of going back if things get too difficult.

Thomas Wolfe said it: "You can't go home again."

But still we try.

KEEPING OUR OPTIONS OPEN

Marital relationships in the nineties have often been referred to as "serial monogamy." People want to keep their options open, to give themselves a back door, to be able to cut and run if seemingly insurmountable obstacles arise. And so, like Dr. Sam Beckett of the television series *Quantum Leap,* we "find ourselves leaping from life to life," not "striving to put right what went wrong," but making sure we can leap out of trouble if the fire gets too hot.

Thus so-called committed relationships are founded on shifting sand. We promise to stay together, not "as long as we both shall *live,*" but "as long as we both shall *love.*" And when the love seems to be fading, we move on to another relationship . . . and a third . . . and a fourth.

We're trying to keep our options open.

In our spiritual life, too, we often try to keep our options open, to be "committed" to God's plan and purposes while still maintaining a tight grip on the reins.

We talk of "absolute surrender" and yet leave the gate unlocked. In the dim recesses of our mind we reassure ourselves with the thought that if this new path with God gets too treacherous, we can always find our way back to the safety of the walled garden again.

But when God calls us out from our safe places — either in initial commitment or in the ongoing challenge of deeper faith — the Lord intends that we face forward resolutely, not looking back or longing for the "good old days" when life seemed easier and the path smoother.

In Genesis 19, Abraham's nephew Lot and his family had found a place to settle — the city of Sodom, known for its reprobate lifestyle and defiance of God. Perhaps Lot mistakenly thought he could make a difference by his example as one of the chosen of God. Perhaps he was just tired of traveling. But whatever the reason, he had become comfortable in Sodom . . . respected, honored for his wisdom, a man of means.

By grace, and because of Abraham's influence, God called Lot and his family to evacuate the city, giving them a chance to save themselves before destruction came upon them. "Flee for your lives!" the angel told them. "Don't look back, and don't stop anywhere in the plain! Flee to the mountains or you will be swept away!" (Genesis 19:17).

After some argument with the angel, Lot took his family and fled. But the ties to their comfortable home were too strong; the temptation was too great: "Lot's wife looked back, and she became a pillar of salt" (Genesis 19:26).

When God leads us out into the unknown — either

protecting us from destruction or moving us into a different realm of fulfillment or a new avenue of service, the temptation to look back will inevitably pull at us. How can we possibly leave behind the secure, familiar place we have known all our life? How can we leave the easy life for the difficult path of change and challenge and growth?

We find ourselves tempted to look over our shoulders to make sure we can still see the path back to the walled garden, back to safety . . . just in case.

But if we look back, we run the risk of being salted: Salted with tears of remorse.

Salt rubbed into the open wound of regret.

The way may look impossible, the mountain path too steep and rocky for our tender feet. But God is leading. And the Spirit says quietly to our heart, *Go forward, upward, onward. Do not look back.*

You can't go home again.

ABANDONING THE SAFETY NET

Anna was a junior in college when she decided to take up gymnastics. She was, frankly, too old to begin such a discipline—gymnasts, after all, usually begin training before they begin elementary school. And she was too big—a tall, muscular young woman who stood five foot ten in her stocking feet.

But Anna was determined. Every day she worked out in the gym, learning the moves, learning how to fall. Then came her first day of trampoline work. Strapped into the harness, she began jumping and tumbling, all the while keeping her eye fixed on the safety net stretched around the edge of the tramp.

She grew bolder. The safety net was there; she couldn't fall off. She took a flying leap and attempted a double somersault in midair. But she only got through one and a half turns.

Anna's head smashed against the edge of the trampoline with a resounding *thud*. Considering the circumstances, she got off lightly: a mild concussion and three weeks in a neck brace.

She had been looking at the safety net, not at her point of landing.

Sometimes for us as Christians, looking for the safety net can be dangerous business.

We seek to follow God along unknown paths, and we trust the Lord as far as we are able. But, whether it is logical or not, we sometimes trust ourselves more. . . .

We trust that we know what is best for us, how much we can handle—when we need to bail out, turn around, and hightail it back down the path to the safety of the walled garden.

We want a back door.

We need a safety net.

But our commitment to God is very much like a lifetime commitment to another person. If we leave ourselves a back door, we will probably use it. If we keep our eye on the safety net, we don't learn to rely on God. If we don't burn our bridges behind us, we will be tempted to cross back over into safer territory.

But we can't go home again.

No matter how agonizing and risky the birth process, the new life must be born. No matter how difficult the questions, the trust level must be forged. No matter how enticing the temptation to go back to the walled garden, the unknown forest must be faced.

If we want to grow, that is.

If we truly want to step out of our comfort zones into the realm of risk and danger, to face the challenges before us and become better, wiser, stronger than we are, we must turn our back on the old ways and face and embrace the new experiences God holds out before us. We must trust the Guardian who leads us . . . without looking back.

In the first stage of John Bunyan's classic, *The Pilgrim's Progress*, the main character (later called Christian) is directed by Evangelist to go through the wicket-gate to begin making his way toward Eternal Life. But as Christian begins his journey, his friends and family try to deter him from his purposes.

They "began to cry after him to return; but the man put his fingers in his ears and ran on, crying 'Life! life! eternal life!' So he looked not behind him . . . but fled towards the middle of the plain."* Like Christian, we have to go forward, no matter what the cost . . . put our fingers in our ears, refuse to look behind us, and run in the direction God is calling us.

We can't go home again.

We can't return to spiritual infancy, allowing others to take up the obligation of meeting our needs. We can't

---

*John Bunyan, *The Pilgrim's Progress* (Philadelphia: J. B. Lippincott & Co., 1877), 15.

retreat to spiritual adolescence, picking and choosing, smorgasbord-style, what responsibilities we are willing to accept. We can't make a day-jaunt into the woods beyond the garden wall and then return to the safety of the fortress-house when night falls and the woods get scary.

Reality lies before us.

We can't go home again.

But we can take home with us.

Home is where we are loved, accepted, freed to be what God has created us to be. Home is where we have room to grow, to change, challenged toward maturity and applauded for our progress.

And when we take the risk to leave the safety and comfort of the familiar, to enter the woods and lock the garden gate behind us, we "come home" in the truest sense imaginable. We come home to a faithful Guardian, a Lord who loves us and is trustworthy in his care for us.

We come home to ourselves.

Come out, the Voice whispers. *There is much you have not seen.*

Come out from your safety into the unknown woods, into the adventure of journeying with God.

Come home to a new way of life, to a higher reality, to new challenges, to a new way of thinking, to a faith that is truly your own. Make your faith walk *personal.*

Guardian is waiting.

Come home.

PART THREE

The Dawn of Trust

Imperceptibly the dawn came, turning the shrouded forest from black to misty gray, then to watercolor pastels. At last the night clouds broke, and a pink-and-orange sunrise threw shafts of light through the trees. Indeed, this was something Quester had never seen before. Her senses were overloaded: the smell of the wet leaves beneath her feet; the rustling sounds of the forest come to life around her and the birds singing overhead; the taste of morning mist on her tongue; the gentle brush of the tall ferns against her face and hands. Never had she felt as *alive* as she did this morning.

"Guardian, this is beautiful!" Quester said, squeezing the hand she still held. She pulled her eyes away from the sunrise and looked toward her companion. Tall and broad-shouldered, he was clad in a gray-blue cloak with a hood drawn low over his forehead. His face was still in the shadows, but his hands were gentle, and every now and then she caught a gleam in his dark eyes.

"Is this worth the risk of leaving your home?" he said, gesturing broadly at the scene before them.

"Yes, Guardian."

"And is this worth the fear you faced last night in the woods?"

"Indeed it is, Guardian."

"Quester, my Child," said Guardian softly, so softly she had to strain to hear him, "can you trust me?"

"Of course I trust you!" Quester responded quickly. "When you called me out, I came. And I followed you here."

"Good," whispered Guardian, "for there is much you have not seen."

CHAPTER SEVEN

The Open Heart

Love is most nearly itself
When here and now cease to matter.
Old men ought to be explorers. . . .
We must be still and still moving
Into another intensity
For a further union, a deeper communion.
　　—T. S. ELIOT

For many years I have worked alone, lived alone, eaten most of my meals at a table for one, and spent the bulk of my time in solitude. For a lot of people I know, that kind of isolation is their best definition of hell. But for me, it worked.

My dog and cat are very respectful of my need for silence. They never complain if I work all night or question me if I take a day off now and then. I set my own schedule, meet my deadlines, and answer to no one except myself.

Now things are about to change. An associate is coming to work with me; her arrival signals a new era in my business, and no doubt some radical changes in other areas of my life as well.

It's time to learn to compromise. . . .

The idea of compromise, I'll admit, came hard at first. When I initially began to recognize the need for help in my home-based business, I balked. I was accustomed to doing things *my* way. But even in the early stages of discussion about the upcoming alliance, I found that my partner had her own ideas about organization and administration . . . and her filing system was certainly far superior to my piling system.

Still, I wasn't sure I wanted to change.

Then one morning, as I was reading Genesis, seven words jumped off the page: "It is not good . . . to be alone" (Genesis 2:18).

For a brief moment or two, I gave in to rationalization. That verse, after all, pertained to God's creation of Eve as a partner for Adam. It referred to marriage, not a business alliance. . . .

Or did it?

In the deep recesses of my soul, I felt a nudge, a breath, a whisper: *You have been alone long enough. Open your heart. . . .*

The Lord was calling me—*me!*—to come out from the safety of my walled garden, to walk into the unknown, to take an enormous risk.

God was asking me to gamble on the truth of my own words.

But I wasn't quite ready to give in.

WHEN HEDGES BECOME FORTRESSES
Open your heart, God repeated.

I quickly framed a rebuttal. "Now, wait a minute . . . what about Proverbs 4:23?" I quoted the passage, as if the Author didn't remember it: "Above all else, guard your heart, for it is the wellspring of life."

It was a verse I had depended upon for a long time. In my early years, I hadn't known how to guard my heart; I wore my emotions outside my skin and endured a great deal of hurt and grief because I was too vulnerable to the manipulations of other people. At long last I was learning to think for myself, to own my own opinions, to trust God and depend upon the Lord for direction and guidance.

And now, as surely as if I had heard the response with my physical ears, my soul resounded with God's reply: *There is a time for building hedges, but when hedges become fortresses, they need to come down.*

The time had come for me to take my own advice: to leave the safety of the walled garden I had created for protection and venture out into the unknown woods beyond . . . led only by the Voice of the One who walked beside me.

Many Christians fall prey to the curse of extremes, just as I had done. When we get hurt because we are too vulnerable, we withdraw and refuse to let anyone come close—even God. When we take risks that don't turn out well, we vow never to risk again. We have difficulty finding that middle ground of wisdom, knowing when to launch out and when to step back; we are as wary as serpents when we need to be as harmless as doves (Matthew 10:16).

CAPPING OFF THE WELLSPRING

Certainly, we want to be careful about guarding our heart. We don't need to be spiritual exhibitionists, letting everyone we meet know the secrets in the deep recesses of our soul. We need to be wise.

But with God, and with carefully selected individuals in our life, openness of heart is necessary . . . and healing . . . and healthy.

To the Samaritan woman at the well, Jesus said, "The water I give . . . will become . . . a spring of water welling up to eternal life" (John 4:14). And to the multitudes at the Feast of Tabernacles, Christ declared, "Whoever believes in me, as the Scripture has said, streams of living water will flow from within him" (John 7:38).

The treasures of our heart, given by the Spirit of God, are not intended to be capped off; that "living water," the "wellspring of life," is a spontaneous cascade of God's grace and love that enriches our own life and flows outward to quench the thirst of those around us.

When we resist God's new directions in our life—new relationships, a change in job or residence, a broadening of attitudes and spiritual perspectives—we shut off the flow of that wellspring of life. We close our heart to the adventure of journeying with Christ.

Once, many years ago, I was part of a local church that was facing some changes and uncertainties in its future. Many of the members resisted the changes, and internal conflict resulted. The pastor, a godly man committed to following the Lord's leading, set aside several Sunday nights for prayer and discussion about the controversy.

Nobody showed up.

Defeated and frustrated, he began to ask various members of the congregation why his attempts at encouraging the church to pray about these issues had failed. The universal response was honest, if deflating: "We had already made up our minds, Pastor. We didn't want to *pray*—and take the chance that God might change what we already believed!"

Openness to God can be unpredictable, even frightening. But when we cap off the wellspring, when we close our heart to the possibility of new directions, we condemn ourselves to a life of stifling sameness. We already know the questions . . . and we are ready with the answers. We see, through tunnel vision, the narrow path we have marked for ourselves . . . and we never catch sight of the glorious variety of God's purposes for our life.

We play it safe, but we miss the larger picture.

We have security within the fortress walls, but we never see the beauty of the woods beyond.

THE INERTIA PRINCIPLE

In order to get my undergraduate degree, I was forced to take college physics—not one of the brighter moments of my academic career, I confess. But I did learn one principle of physics that made sense to me: the *principle of inertia.* According to this concept, "a body at rest tends to remain at rest." This idea was not intended to apply to my attendance record for early morning classes, although sometimes the principle fit. Rather, the concept of inertia pertains to the resistance that must be overcome to get a "body at rest" in motion . . . to get a couch potato up and onto the exercise bike.

In spiritual terms, too, a soul at rest tends to remain at rest. To get ourselves moving in a different direction, we often have to overcome a great deal of resistance—

as I did when I came to grips with God's new directive
for my life and work. We quote a verse: "I the Lord do
not change" (Malachi 3:6) — and make a cognitive leap
to the conclusion that therefore we, also, do not need to
change . . . we simply have to find God's will and sit
down. We sing "Great Is Thy Faithfulness," and when
we come to the line "Thou changest not," we assume
that the divine characteristic of immutability applies to
the Lord's guidance in the spiritual journey.

But *does* God change?

Does God lead us down one path at one time, and then
alter the direction?

Can the hedges we build to guard our heart become
fortresses that must be broken down if we are to follow
the Voice that calls us out?

One intriguing, baffling story in the Bible helps us
come to grips with the changes that are possible when the
Lord is in control. Peter, the leader of the disciples after
Christ's ascension, is a devout, law-abiding Jew . . . so
devout that he requires new converts to Christianity to
be circumcised and observe the Jewish law.

Then the Lord makes an astounding, unorthodox
move. God speaks to a *Gentile* named Cornelius — a
Roman centurion, no less!* The Spirit instructs this God-
fearing Gentile to call for Peter so that Cornelius and his
family can hear the word of the Lord.

Meanwhile, God is preparing an object lesson for Peter.
As the apostle is praying on the roof of a house, hungry
and waiting for dinner, he sees a vision in which heaven

*The story of Cornelius, and of Peter's confrontation with God, is found in
Acts 10.

opens and he is presented with all variety of unclean animals. The Lord tells him, "Rise, Peter, kill and eat."

But Peter refuses. This isn't part of the game plan; he has always limited himself to a kosher diet, according to the laws of Moses. "Surely not, Lord!" Peter replies vehemently. "I have never eaten anything impure or unclean."

Then God speaks a word of reprimand that changes Peter's life and attitudes forever: "Do not call anything impure that God has made clean" (Acts 10:15).

The Lord's *character* does not change, but sometimes God's *leading* does. Sometimes God alters the path, reverses direction, opens up a new way before us . . . a way we have never imagined, a way we would never have chosen for ourselves.

And to respond to God's new directions, we must set aside our resistance.

We must overcome inertia.

We must open our heart.

OPEN-HEART SURGERY

The last time I had a physical examination, the doctor told me that I have a heart murmur. "It's nothing to worry about," he said. "It's a prolapsed mitral valve, which means that the valve doesn't close completely when the blood pumps through. It won't kill you, but it may cause fatigue and slow you down."

And I wondered: *Do I have a murmuring heart against God?*

When the Lord calls me to change, does my heart resist moving in a different direction than the way God has led me in the past?

Does my heart murmur result in fatigue of the soul? Does it make me drag my feet, reticent to follow eagerly when the Lord indicates that change is coming?

A spiritual heart murmur won't kill us, but it certainly slows us down.

If we live, like Peter, with preconceived notions that the way God has operated in the past is the way it will always be . . .

If we assume that we can sit down in the will of God and never be disturbed again . . .

If we mutter and murmur and resist and argue when the Lord opens up a new path before us . . .

If we let spiritual inertia rule us . . .

We will never know the joy of a heart poised and ready to hear the Voice of our Guardian, to follow in the new way through the unfamiliar forest of our spiritual journey. God may want to lead us in a different way, down unfamiliar trails, toward a difficult mountain pass or across rugged terrain. Our heart needs to be ready — strong and exercised and willing to face the challenges that lie before us.

We need healthy hearts, and open hearts.

PRIMING THE PUMP

I once heard the story of an old miner out in the desert. Thirsty and weary, he came upon a well with an ancient, rusted pump. Attached to the pump handle was a crudely lettered note:

This here pump will work just fine, but ya gotta prime it first. There's a can of water under the handle. Don't drink it, even if you're powerful thirsty. Use it to prime the pump, and you'll get all the water you need. But when you're done, don't forget to fill the priming can for the next guy.

The miner was, indeed, "powerful thirsty," and from the looks of the pump, he doubted that he'd get any water at all out of it. He found the priming can; it was full. Although the water inside was stagnant and smelly, he battled against the temptation to drink the water in hand rather than risk it on the possibility of a dry well.

Over and over he read the words "Prime the pump, and you'll get all the water you need." His mind rebelled at the foolishness of the idea, but his heart was drawn by the promise.

At last he followed his heart.

He poured the stagnant contents of the priming can into the mechanism of the pump—every drop of it. Then he closed his eyes and began to heave on the pump handle. Nothing happened; the old pump groaned and creaked, and the miner cursed himself for his stupidity. He had been right all along; the well was dry.

Then, just as he was about to give up, he felt the suction of the pump take hold, and out flowed fresh water, cool and clear—enough to quench his thirst, enough for his horse, enough to fill his water bags . . . enough to take a bath in, if he had wanted to.

Refreshed and supplied, the miner went on his way— but not before he had refilled the priming can, capped it, and set it back in its place. Someone else would come this way, needing water . . . and if he had the courage to risk the contents of the priming can, he would find more than he bargained for.

Having an open heart to God's leading primes the pump. There is risk, certainly—the peril of change, the hazard of loss, the possibility that the path may be a dead end, that the well may be dry.

But if we take the chance, if we risk opening our heart and trusting God, we too may find more than we bargained for. We may find grace and joy and adventure— enough to quench our thirst, enough to share with fellow travelers.

When we abandon our claim to the water in hand . . . when we clench our teeth and pour out the contents of the priming can, we give up the security of the known for the possibility that lies ahead in the unknown. We use up what we have to invest it in the future . . . we shut the door behind us, lock the gate, and go forward into the unfamiliar forest.

Prime the pump, and you'll get all the water you need. Open your heart, and the wellsprings of life will flow.

CHAPTER EIGHT

The Searching Mind

What you thought you came for
Is only a shell, a husk of meaning
From which the purpose breaks only when it is fulfilled
If at all. Either you had no purpose
Or the purpose is beyond the end you figured
And is altered in fulfillment.
    —T. S. ELIOT

In *The Last Battle*—the final book of C. S. Lewis's classic children's series The Chronicles of Narnia—Peter, Lucy, and the other children are ushered through a magical stable door into Narnia, the world ruled by the great lion Aslan. Beyond the door they find a land full of beauty and majesty, a true heaven where goodness reigns and no evil exists. It is the world they have been searching for all their lives.

But they find something else there . . . something that surprises and confuses them. Along with all the creatures who have served Aslan faithfully and fought for the cause of right, they come upon someone they never expected to find in Narnia . . . one who had formerly been an enemy of Aslan.

This young "enemy," however, has lived his life in a search for truth. He didn't *know* he was searching for Aslan, but he was. And the great Lion tells him:

> Beloved, unless thy desire had been for me thou wouldst not have sought so long and so truly. For all find what they truly seek.*

All find what they truly seek. For many of us, this seems a difficult concept . . . even a heretical one. We are conditioned to believe that we must *know* what we seek in order to find it . . . that we must first *understand* the nature of the journey before we set out in our quest toward spiritual enlightenment. And, from a judgmental perspective, we sometimes condemn those who are "looking in the wrong place" to a life of darkness and unfulfillment.

The problem is, we have misinterpreted and misapplied the scriptural injunction "Seek and you will find" (Luke 11:9). We assume that God pauses at the doorstep of our heart, hoping that we will say the magic words to open the door. Doesn't the Lord, after all, wait to be invited in? And if "all find what they truly seek," shouldn't we be actively seeking God's presence and work in our life?

That depends, I suppose, on what we are searching for, and why.

If we are seeking some mystical, miraculous experience

---

*C. S. Lewis, *The Last Battle* (New York: Macmillan Publishing Co., 1976), 165.

of God, depending upon our feelings or our perceptions to carry us to a higher level of spirituality, we may be sadly disappointed. If we are seeking intellectual understanding of the ways of the Lord, answers to all our questions, or ammunition to blast away at others' erroneous perceptions of God, we may find ourselves shaking our fists in frustration toward a heaven that has clanged shut like an iron door.

God does work miracles in our life, of course; God still reaches into our heart to reveal the divine nature to us. God does, sometimes, give us answers to our questions and aid our intellectual understanding. But our seeking for God needs to go beyond what the Lord can *do* in our life, deep into the realms of who God *is*.

We need to allow God to be present in all our circumstances.

We need to abandon our preconceived notions of what we think God should do in any given situation.

We need to seek God for *God's* sake.

"SURELY THE LORD IS IN THIS PLACE."

As I look back on my own journey of faith, I notice an odd kind of correlation: Often God has been most intensively at work in my life when I was totally unaware of the Lord's presence. Often I have *thought* I understood God's purposes and directions in my life; I have, over the years, sought to discipline my mind to search for truth. And yet my greatest experiences of spiritual deepening seem to have come when I understood nothing of what God was doing.

A few years ago, at a silent retreat, I made this amazing

discovery. As part of my personal search, I created a line graph that traced the high and low points of my life over the past five years . . . those times when I felt happy and content, those times when I felt troubled and in turmoil. Then, superimposed over the first graph, I drew a second line in red—a line that represented, from the wonderfully clear perspective of hindsight, just how and when God had been most actively at work in the maturing process of my faith. Ironically, those points of my life that *seemed* the lowest were the very times God had been working to bring change and growth in my soul. And I felt like Jacob awakening from his dream at Bethel: "Surely the Lord is in this place, and I was not aware of it" (Genesis 28:16).

But how can God be at work when we are not aware of it?

It's called *grace.*

Grace can be a hard dose of reality for those of us who are accustomed to paying our own way, to pulling ourselves up by our bootstraps, to earning a living by the sweat of our brow. Acknowledging grace means recognizing that I am not self-sufficient, that I have needs—deep needs for spiritual direction and meaning and significance for my life—and that I don't even know what to seek . . . or how. Receiving grace means accepting what I have not earned—indeed, embracing something I didn't even know I lacked.

My mother's wry sense of humor has helped me to learn an important lesson about grace. Every Christmas, at least one package arrives with the label "You don't know you want this, but you do."

So it is with grace, with God's direction in our life. Circumstances change, and we resist the changes. Life moves on, but we want to stay where we are comfortable. And gently, with a smile, God says, "Follow me. Come out; there is much you have not seen. You don't know you want this, but you do."

A Mind Is a Terrible Thing to Waste

For years the United Negro College Fund had as its motto A Mind Is a Terrible Thing to Waste. But Christians sometimes waste their minds by not *thinkng* about their faith, by not coupling reason with Spirit. Despite our insistence upon knowing exactly what we are searching for, we nevertheless assume, "Faith only welcome here. Leave your mind at the door."

God, however, seems to have a different perspective. Three times the Scripture records Jesus responding to the question "What is the greatest commandment?" And each time his answer is the same:

"Love the Lord your God with all your heart and with all your soul and with all your mind and with all your strength" (Mark 12:30).*

But we're not very adept at loving God with our mind. In fact, many of us have been taught that thinking is incompatible with faith, that we can't reason our way toward God, that intellect simply gets in the way of believing.

And those of us who insist upon using our mind any-way often struggle with the opposite temptation — trying

*Similar answers appear in Matthew 22:37 and Luke 10:27, and all of these responses refer back to the Old Testament injunction of Deuteronomy 6:4-5.

to understand everything. We fall into the trap of attempting to codify the works of the Spirit into an easily accessible system, so that God becomes predictable and consistent, and we know ahead of time what the Lord's response will be. Statistical probability takes the place of faith, and logic replaces love.

Yet faith—true faith, the kind God honors—includes the searching of the mind as well as the devotion of the heart. In the book of Acts, the church at Berea was applauded for its analytical approach to accepting the Good News: "The Bereans were of more noble character . . . for they received the message with great eagerness and examined the Scriptures every day to see if what Paul said was true" (Acts 17:11).

God doesn't tell us to leave our mind at the door. Like the Bereans, we are called to *use* our mind . . . to investigate, to question, to examine the Scriptures. We are not required to swallow everything we have been taught, hook, line, and sinker, to become just another mounted trophy on the Great Fisherman's mantel.

We are called to follow, but we are also called—miracle of miracles!—to *think*.

God has not only equipped us with brains but also placed us in a world rich with natural beauty, scientific wonders, art and music, poetry and song. We can experience God's gentleness in a summer breeze, God's majesty and power in a thunderstorm. We can discover God's measureless intricacy through science as well as Scripture, and absorb theology from Milton as well as from Moses. The Lord has provided us with an infinite variety of source material from which we can learn about ourselves, about others, and about the One who created us in the divine image.

Our search for a deeper intimacy with God is not so much a treasure hunt for the right answers or the proper theology as a progressive movement toward openness to the Lord's purposes in our life, a journey toward *knowing God* rather than simply knowing facts *about* God. Asking questions, examining what we believe and why, even doubting what we have been taught . . . all are legitimate avenues for the mind that searches for truth.

Pilate asked, "What is truth?" but he didn't wait around for an answer. Truth was standing right in front of him, in the person of Jesus Christ, and yet Pilate's eyes were closed to the reality of who Christ was. He was blinded by his own preconceived notions, by the pressure of society, by the expectations of those in authority. He asked the right question, but his mind was not open to the answer.

If we truly desire to have a fully developed faith, we must search with our mind as well as our heart.

The psalmist David gives us a clue to the real priorities on God's heart. He identifies the "one thing" that the soul open to God truly desires:

> One thing I ask of the Lord, this is what I seek: that I may dwell in the house of the Lord all the days of my life, to gaze upon the beauty of the Lord and to seek him in his temple. (Psalm 27:4)

Jesus recognized a similar desire in the heart of Mary

of Bethany. Pressured by her sister Martha to quit sitting around listening to Christ and get to work, Mary refused. She sat steadfastly at the Messiah's feet and drank in his words of comfort and hope. And Jesus said, "Only one thing is needed. Mary has chosen what is better, and it will not be taken away from her" (Luke 10:42).

One thing I ask of the Lord . . . one thing is needful.
One thing.
God.

What You Thought You Came For

When we embark on the search for a deeper, more meaningful relationship with God, we may be expecting some kind of earthshaking sense of God's presence with us. We may be hoping for profound spiritual enlightenment, for answers to our questions, for a Mount of Transfiguration revelation.

God, however, may have something quite different in mind.

T. S. Eliot, in his masterpiece, *The Four Quartets*, gives us a startling glimpse into the purposes of God for our searching:

> *What you thought you came for*
> *Is only a shell, a husk of meaning*
> *From which the real purpose breaks only when it is fulfilled*
> *If at all. Either you had no purpose*
> *Or the purpose is beyond the end you figured*
> *And is altered in fulfillment.**

*T. S. Eliot, "Little Gidding," from *The Four Quartets*, in *The Complete Poems and Plays of T. S. Eliot* (New York: Harcourt, Brace, & World, Inc., 1971), 139.

When we step out and take the hand of our Guardian, leaving behind what we have known and venturing into the unfamiliar woods beyond the wall, we may *think* we know the purpose for which we have been called out. We may *believe* that we understand what we need in our spiritual life, where we are going on the journey. But God may have a different plan, a "purpose . . . beyond the end you figured."

We are called to seek. But for all our knowledge and understanding, we may find ourselves seeking something that is totally unknown to us. What we "thought [we] came for" may be "only a shell, a husk of meaning." Often, when we find a place of deeper understanding, we discover that the purpose of our search—the one we thought we understood—has been changed in the process. But whether we understand or not, God uses our searching mind to lead us out, out to where the real purpose breaks forth as it is fulfilled in us.

Sometimes, in hindsight, we can see the direction of our searching. In other instances we never know the real reasons for the journey . . . except for the ultimate reason, a more intimate relationship with God. But always, God is present, drawing us, urging us to go deeper, to explore further, to discover more.

We may not find what we thought we came for. We may come to realize that God will not be forced into a prefabricated mold of predictable responses. We may end up with more questions than answers.

But we will be changed.

When we open our mind to search for the truth that lies in God, we discover what we need to know. We learn to depend upon the understanding of the One who has called us out rather than upon ourselves. Our faith, refined in the fires of questioning and struggle, becomes our own.

We learn to lean upon grace.

Guardian calls us out . . . every one of us, into the unknown, where our answers no longer work and we must use our mind as well as our heart.

The purpose is beyond the end you figured.

You don't know you want this, but you do.

God is in this place, even when you are unaware of it.

CHAPTER NINE

The Vulnerable Soul

For most of us, there is only the unattended
Moment. . . .
music heard so deeply
That it is not heard at all.
  —T. S. ELIOT

Ten weeks ago, between the evening news and the Thursday Night Movie, my business partner's cat, who was visiting for a while, gave birth to four kittens in my upstairs bathtub.

I watched, enthralled, as these tiny new lives struggled their way into the world. With their eyes closed tight and their ears flapped over and their little legs weak and useless, they were totally vulnerable, wholly dependent upon the one who had given birth to them.

Then something very strange happened.

The mother cat, a beautiful, gentle-spirited, purring Himalayan named Bronte, transformed into a snarling, hissing, growling attack cat. She lunged at anything that came near—my dog, my leg, my four-year-old Siamese/Angora, who was understandably curious but not at all threatening.

At first Bronte only defended her bathtub turf. But soon her defense strategy extended further. She would jump out of the bathtub and race down the hall to assault the poor confused dog from behind . . . as if a civilized, ancient, kitty-loving Sheltie had plans to serve up her brood for breakfast.

However irritating Bronte's behavior might have been at the time, she was only doing her job. She was protecting her vulnerable litter; she probably would have died before she let anyone or anything hurt those kittens.

And the babies? They seemed blissfully unaware of the lengths to which their mother went to protect them. They just wanted to eat and sleep and grow and climb the lace curtains and do all that important kitten stuff. I doubt that they ever even said, "Thanks, Mom."

THE KITTEN PHASE

At various times in our journey with God, we go through what I call the *kitten phase.* We discover some new truth about ourselves, about our life with the Lord, about the beauty and wonder of the universe, or of God's grace toward us. We become like kittens—enthusiastic, delighted, overcome with the joys and marvels of life. We want to explore, to climb and jump and run at breakneck speed, to slide on the rugs and dive into the laundry basket—to see how far, how fast, how high we can go.

Then the mother-cat nature kicks in.

We pull back; we force ourselves to *calm down,* to *be dignified,* to regain our composure. We make ourselves grow up.

We want to protect ourselves. . . .

So we shut down. And we lose the joy of that wonder, that vulnerability.

It's a difficult dilemma. How can we take responsibility for our own life and yet allow ourselves to revel in the joy of discovery? How can we be wise about guarding our heart and still be vulnerable enough to experience the wonder along the way?

We have forgotten, it seems, that there is a time for everything—a time to weep and a time to laugh, a time to mourn and a time to dance . . . a time to be the protective mother and a time to be the vulnerable kitten, unafraid and undaunted.

We don't remember—or if we remember, we push the truth aside—that being kittenlike *is the kitten's job,* at least for the present. The running, the stalking, the chasing of tails and jumping on siblings from a hiding place . . . all that activity is training ground for adult cat behavior, discipline for the hunt, education for adult responsibilities. Kitten play is the feline *McGuffey's Reader,* the primer for what is to come in the future.

As humans—and more important, as humans on a quest for deeper spirituality—the kitten phase, the time of innocence and wonder, is vitally important to our relationship with God . . . and our understanding of ourselves. There may be times when we need to cover ourselves with a shell of protection. But in our journey of discovery with God, we also need to cultivate spiritual vulnerability.

THE DANCE OF SHAMELESS JOY

When King David returned from battle, bringing the ark of the covenant back to its rightful home among

God's chosen people, he was completely overcome with the joy of the moment. In the presence of God and all the nation of Israel, he threw off his royal robes and danced before the Lord . . . a dance of holy abandon, of shameless joy. And God, apparently, was pleased with David's uninhibited demonstration of exhilaration.

David's wife Michal, however, had a different response.

This was, after all, the king of Israel. He should know better. He should have more sense of dignity, of decorum. Michal stood at the window and watched David dance, and as he leaped for pure joy, her soul grew brittle with disdain and criticism. "She despised him in her heart" (2 Samuel 6:16).

When David returned home that night, Michal was waiting for him, ready with a caustic response: "How the king of Israel has distinguished himself today, disrobing in the sight of the slave girls of his servants as any vulgar fellow would!" (2 Samuel 6:20).

Michal had no heart to share in the joy of God's victory on that day. Embarrassed and offended by her husband's display of enthusiasm before the Lord, she tried to shame him, to shut down the vulnerability of a soul open to God.

God saw her heart. God heard her shaming words. And, just as her soul was closed to the Lord, from that day on, her womb was also closed. Michal remained barren for the rest of her life.

STILLING THE MICHAL VOICE

All of us have a "Michal voice" inside us . . . the mother-cat protectiveness that warns our kitten soul, "Calm down; be dignified; don't be too vulnerable."

And we have a "David voice" as well . . . the voice that tells us, "Open up; be not ashamed; dance with joy before your Lord."

For most of my life I have struggled with the conflict between these two voices—what psychologists sometimes refer to as the natural self and the adaptive self. My natural self, the David voice, is open, creative, trusting, loving, and enthusiastic. But my adaptive self, conditioned by years of trying to please other people and find approval in the acceptance of those around me, tends to be fearful, insecure, and self-protective. That is my Michal voice. I'm working on it, but frankly, I'm still not very adept at silencing the Michal voice and giving freedom to the David voice.

Like many adults, I have difficulty balancing the desire to be a "grown-up" with the beauty, wonder, and loveliness of the childlike soul. I shrink from dancing before the Lord because I know that Michal stands at the window, looking down on me with disdain.

We do, after all, need to become adults, to take responsibility for ourselves, to own our own opinions, to make our own decisions. When Guardian's Voice calls us to venture into the woods beyond the wall, we leave behind the protections of our fortress-home and the safe, cultivated gardens of our childhood. We take a risk. In spiritual terms, we begin to grow up.

But we often misinterpret what it means to grow up. We mistakenly think that in order to become spiritual adults, we must leave behind all the wonder and magic, the joy and abandonment, the fantasy and mystery of a soul open and vulnerable to the ways of

God. We become hardened, skeptical, cynical . . . and barren.

We need to learn—again and again, at each new turn in the road—how to silence the Michal voice and give ourselves wholeheartedly to the adventure of spiritual journeying.

BECOMING AS A LITTLE CHILD

My friend Joy, age eight, told on me last week. I had been consciously trying to cultivate the natural self, to allow my soul to open up, to learn to play, to recapture some of the wonder I lost somewhere along the way during my formative years. Joy was helping.

One evening we convened at the kitchen table with coloring books, crayons, and two bottles of bubbles. For a while we blew bubbles . . . or, rather, she blew bubbles and I blew soapy residue all over the kitchen floor. Then we sat down to color. But the adult anxieties of my life—deadlines, workload, stress, and internal changes—just wouldn't seem to go away. Finally, a little exasperated with my inability to enjoy myself, Joy turned to me and whispered, "It's OK to go outside the lines, you know."

The next day she confided to a mutual friend, "Penny's been trying to learn how to play, but she isn't very good at it yet."

She was right. I wasn't very good at it. I was trying . . . watching the kittens leap fearlessly from the back of the wing chairs and skitter across the room . . . listening to the voice that told me, "It's OK to color outside the lines." But somehow, deep in the recesses of my adult soul, I had a hard time flinging off my cumbersome robes to join the dance of shameless joy. Michal still stood at the window with her hands on her hips, judging, criticizing, shaming.

Jesus said, "I tell you the truth, unless you change and become like little children, you will never enter the kingdom of heaven" (Matthew 18:3).

It's not a threat. It's a principle.

Children trust. They are open and receptive and accepting.

Children absorb. Their eyes are wide to the world around them.

Children change. They grow; they develop; they form opinions, then change their mind.

Children love. They give themselves unreservedly to those who have earned their respect and affection.

Children are wise. Instinctively, they can spot a phony in a second, but still they do not lose their childlike wonder, awe, and faith.

When Christ expresses the "child-faith" principle of entering the kingdom, I believe he refers to those attributes of childlikeness that balance our "adult" approach to life:

Questioning without cynicism.

Enthusiasm without concern for appearances.

Exploration without fear.

Failure without regret.

Vulnerability of soul that renders us open to joy, to trust, to true faith in One who can be counted on to be faithful.

But how can I become like a little child again? How, with all my adult baggage, can I enter into the journey with joyful abandon and face the future as an adventure rather than a threat? How can I respond with enthusiasm when my Guardian says to me, "Come out; there is much you have not seen"?

I can keep my eyes focused on the source of my joy.

LOOKING IN THE RIGHT DIRECTION

My latest concession to middle age came this summer when I went to have my eyes examined. As I feared, the time of bifocals was upon me. Close work, astigmatism, and a lifetime addiction to reading had taken their toll.

"You shouldn't have much trouble adjusting to these," the optometrist said when she fitted my new glasses. "But remember, you'll have to look directly at whatever you're focusing on. Your vision will be blurred on the sides. As long as you focus straight ahead, you won't have any problem."

As long as you focus straight ahead . . .

It's a good principle. Choose a desk on the first row in the classroom, and your grades will probably improve. Sit in the pews near the front—they're almost always empty—and you won't be distracted by the constant activity in the rear of the sanctuary. Focus straight ahead, and your vision will be clearer.

The writer of Hebrews put it this way: "Let us fix our eyes on Jesus, the author and perfecter of our faith" (Hebrews 12:2).

When David threw aside his robes and danced with jubilation before the Lord, his eyes were fixed on God alone. Had he looked aside, up to the window where Michal stood with a condemning frown on her face, he

might have been distracted from the glorious abandonment of the moment. He might have sensed her judgment, her disapproval, and felt compelled to put a lid on
his uninhibited worship.

But he didn't.

He flung aside the conventions of religious propriety
and went on leaping in the presence of the Lord.

He focused on God, and let the chips of his wife's
criticism fall around his head. He refused to let someone
else's attitude rob his joy or steal from the offering of
adoration he had reserved for God.

He turned a deaf ear to the Michal voice, and danced on.

When Guardian's whisper calls us out, into the woods
beyond the wall, into the place of unknown challenges
and delights, we need to do what David did. We need to
fix our eyes on the One who calls us, and dance with all
our might.

Never mind the critical voices that urge us to be dignified, to remember our place, to refrain from showing too
much excitement. There is a time for everything . . . and
there will be time enough for restraint.

Never mind the nagging words that haunt us, telling us
that someone, somewhere, might disapprove of our
wholehearted abandonment to God's new directions for
our life.

Never mind the warning, true though it may be, that
mourning might wait just around the bend.

Guardian stands with one hand outstretched, waiting
to lead us to the adventure that waits in the woods
beyond the wall.

This is the kitten phase.

This is the day of discovery.

This is the time for shameless joy.

Now, today, while the sun dawns bright in the eastern sky and life is full of wonder and promise . . .

Dance for all you're worth.

PART FOUR

On the Mountains of Delight

For many months Quester and Guardian walked, slept under the stars, ate the fruit that grew in abundance in the forest, and encountered many new and lovely wonders. She watched the flight of an eagle from the cliffs overlooking the sea, saw the blue whales breach in the bay. Once, for a whole morning, she sat in the shallows and pondered the activity of a hermit crab as he scuttled along the sandy ocean bottom. Quester and Guardian climbed the rocky mountainside with a herd of goats and stood on the peak overlooking their universe. And always, Guardian was with her, her companion, protector, and friend.

Then one morning, Guardian drew her aside and pulled

a small, worn book from beneath the folds of his cloak. "I have a gift for you, Child," he said.

Quester took the book in her hands and examined it carefully. She had never seen such a lovely volume. The cover was crafted of deep bloodred leather, illuminated around the spine with gold scrollwork; and the pages were edged with gilt. Wonder washed over her as she held it in her hands and breathed the deep musty fragrance of antique leather and ancient ink.

"Open it," Guardian said quietly.

With trembling hands, as if she knew she held a priceless treasure, Quester turned to the flyleaf. Written in a bold, graceful hand, the inscription read, *For the one who sought me and has found me. I am yours forever, and you are mine.*

It was a book of love poems, penned through the ages by people whose names she did not recognize. But to Quester, every poem seemed written especially for her by Guardian himself. Her heart thrilled with the movement of the verses, flying, soaring, singing out Guardian's love for her.

Quester would sit for hours, immersed in the book, reading aloud to herself the words that stirred her own heart to a love deeper than she had ever thought possible.

She wrote long pages of response to Guardian's love, poems of her own celebrating her choice to follow him, and his faithfulness to her.

At first it seemed a silly, pointless exercise—after all, he was right there with her. But he didn't seem to begrudge the time she spent reading and writing; in fact, he seemed to enjoy it. Quester could almost feel his eyes watching her as she read and meditated and wrote her poems. Somehow, without words, she could sense his pleasure in her joy.

Occasionally, when she was reading an especially touching poem or reaching deep into herself for a response, Quester would experience a twinge of melancholy, a deep sadness. Her mind would flash back to her days before meeting Guardian, how she had been kept imprisoned within her walled garden—imprisoned not by force, but by her own fears. And briefly, just briefly, she would lament the lost years when she hadn't known what she was missing.

Before she met Guardian, Quester had never realized that she had been lonely. She had always assumed that her life was rather like anyone else's. Now she knew, and in knowing her former aloneness, knew also the full joy of Guardian's love and companionship. She was happy for the first time in her life, and she was convinced that nothing—nothing—could ever tarnish that happiness.

CHAPTER TEN

The Call to Exploration

Fare forward, you who think that you are voyaging;
You are not those who saw the harbour
Receding, or those who will disembark . . .
And do not think of the fruit of action.
Fare forward.
　—T. S. ELIOT

When I was about ten, my parents and brother and I took a family vacation to Arkansas — a week-long adventure to explore the breathtaking scenery, interesting little hidden-away villages, and unusual attractions of the Ozarks.

It was an adventure, all right.

The resort owner had obviously spent most of his ready cash on the miracle-working photographer who planned the layout for the brochure. Our "luxury accommodations" on a "beautiful Alpine lake" turned out to be a vermin-infested, two-room cabin on an oversized catfish pond. For my mother, whose idea of "roughing it" is a ten-year-old Holiday Inn, it was pure torture.

After two days of battling spiders, roaches, and the

insidious red sand from the "beach," we abandoned nature and went in search of a clean bathroom and air-conditioning. We were determined to redeem this holiday from total disaster.

As we drove, we began to pass signs advertising "the most fascinating cave this side of Carlsbad Caverns." Ah, this was it—something *interesting* to do.

My mother, who only wanted a little peace and quiet, declared that she would stay outside, find a shady spot, and read while we explored the caverns. But when we emerged an hour and a half later, we found her sitting on a rock, cradling her left arm gingerly, her face pale and clammy.

She, too, had gone exploring. As she sat and took in the beautiful woodland scenery, she noticed a hole, high up on the side of the mountain. If she could just get up there, she might be able to peer in and see inside the cave from a little different vantage point. On the way down, she had slipped and fallen. She was all right, she insisted.

As it turned out, she had broken her arm.

We never let her live it down, of course—for years the story has been told and retold at family gatherings . . . how Mother wouldn't pay three dollars for a tour of the cave, but tried to find her own way in when no one was looking.

And she responds, "Oh, but it was worth it! I *did* get to see in, and it was quite an adventure."

EXPLORING SOULS

We all have that yearning to explore, the inner urge to see and know . . . the force that drove my mother to defy gravity and common sense and scale the side of a mountain to see what was in the cave.

We are called to be explorers.

As children—and sometimes as adults, as in my mother's case—exploring can get us into a lot of trouble. Babies grab and chew on anything they can reach with their chubby little paws: Mommy's earring, Daddy's nose, the cat's tail, the bleaching cleanser under the kitchen sink. Toddlers pull books and lamps and tables down on their heads; preschoolers wander away from home because the sparkles on the creek are just too enticing to resist. Teenagers experiment with fads and foolishness, trying on and discarding a different personality every week in an attempt to find the one that fits.

Exploring can be dangerous.

Christopher Columbus, after all, could have been wrong. He could have fallen off the end of the world and been eaten by sea monsters.

Ruth, in following Naomi back to Bethlehem, could have ended her life in poverty and barrenness.

The people of Israel could have died in the desert and put an end to Judeo-Christian history as we know it.

Mary the mother of Christ could have ended up as an outcast with an illegitimate son—or even stoned to death. . . .

It's risky to explore, to reach out beyond ourselves, to seek deeper knowledge and understanding, to go further in our relationship with God. It's not safe to push at the boundaries, to ask questions, to take the next step into the great unknown.

Why, then, do we do it? Why should we? Isn't discretion the better part of valor? Isn't it more prudent to stay where we're secure, where we are guarded and protected, shielded from broken arms and battered hearts and souls that struggle with questions our mind cannot comprehend?

Of course it is.

It's safer to hole up where we are, where we know the rules and are sheltered from the storms. It's safer not to ask questions, not to explore the glorious possibilities of life in a different realm from the one we presently know. It's safer not to launch out in the deeps, where dragons dwell.

It's safer, for that matter, to stay in the womb.

The problem is, we're not made that way.

We're made to be explorers.

INQUIRING MINDS

For the spiritual traveler, the voyage into uncharted waters is a journey of discovery primarily for the mind and spirit rather than for the physical self. Sometimes, of course, we are called to radical changes in profession, lifestyle, or location. But the more important changes, the more vital deepening process, occur within us rather than on the outside.

From the moment of birth, perhaps even from the moment of conception, human beings are driven by the compulsion to investigate, to reach out beyond themselves, to discover just what kind of world they live in, and what kind of people they are going to become. The process is called *thinking*, and although it is a difficult challenge sometimes, it is essential for our development as human beings . . . and as spiritual beings.

The physical growth process in a human child takes somewhere between fifteen and eighteen years. But anyone who has lived with a teenager knows that the process isn't nearly over with the completion of puberty. It takes many, many more years in our society before that child is fully grown, functioning with adult reasoning and taking on adult responsibilities.

It's rather like building a house. Once the foundations are in, the walls and roof put up, and the wiring and plumbing in place, we could, conceivably, declare that the house is finished and move right in. But there is more — much more — to do.

In fact, even after the carpets are laid, the interior walls papered, the kitchen cabinets arranged, and the furniture brought in, we still spend a great deal of time and money to make it what we want it to be. The process never ends. We're forever putting in new shrubbery, redecorating, hanging curtains, rearranging furniture . . . or, at the very least, vacuuming carpets and scrubbing bathtubs and replacing light bulbs.

Why, then, do we fail to recognize that building our *interior* home, which is much more important than the roof over our heads, is also an ongoing, lifelong process? We move, we change, we grow, we rearrange; sometimes we even knock out a wall and add on. But we do not stay the same.

Instinctive reasoning, put in us by a God who loves us and wants the best for us, constrains us to confront the hard realities of life — to stand and walk when we'd be more comfortable crawling; to embrace the traumas of adolescence when we'd much rather stay in childhood; to

face the challenges of adult life when it would be easier
to let someone else care for our needs.

Sadly, in this fallen world of ours, some people do
grow to physical adulthood while their mind remains
behind in infancy. Individuals challenged by mental retardation have their own gifts to offer those who love them,
but they will never become the complete adults they were
intended to be. They have no choice.

In spiritual terms, however, most of us do have a
choice. We do not have to give in to spiritual retardation,
to the internal atrophy that locks us into a preestablished
mode of opinion or behavior.

We can think for ourselves.

We can listen to the One who calls us out.

We can explore new directions in the journey of the heart.

Paul, in his letter to the Corinthians—a church that
proudly boasted of its many spiritual gifts—reprimands
the believers for allowing themselves to continue in spiritual infancy:

> Brothers and sisters, I could not speak to you as
> spiritual people, but rather as people of the flesh, as
> infants in Christ. I fed you with milk, not solid food,
> for you were not ready for solid food. Even now you
> are still not ready, for . . . there is jealousy and quar-
> reling among you. (1 Corinthians 3:1-3, NRSV)

In a similar vein, the writer of Hebrews says:

> You have become dull in understanding. For though
> by this time you ought to be teachers, you need

someone to teach you again the basic elements of the oracles of God. You need milk, not solid food; for everyone who lives on milk, being still an infant, is unskilled in the word of righteousness. But solid food is for the mature, for those whose faculties have been trained by practice to distinguish good from evil. (Hebrews 5:11-14, NRSV)

All too easily we can become "dull in understanding," spiritually and intellectually calcified, withered in soul and content to stay that way. We can actually come to a place where we think we understand all we need to know—about God, about ourselves, about faith.

Sometimes the religious establishment around us tacitly encourages such spiritual retardation. And after we've run up against resistance a few times, we decide that it's easier not to have our cages rattled; it's safer to keep our carefully constructed protective barriers in place. Often without realizing it, we set our shoes in concrete and sing, "We shall not be moved."

But when we respond to the call to leave the walled garden and venture out into the woods beyond, we take the gamble of having our preconceived notions shattered. We open ourselves to new truth and new ways of perceiving; we embrace "the removing of what can be shaken . . . so that what cannot be shaken may remain" (Hebrews 12:27). We commit ourselves to exploration.

And, if we are realists, we launch out with open eyes, knowing that we may get some bruises—even a broken bone or two—along the way. But the adventure of life is worth the risk of leaving the womb.

"Stop thinking like children," Paul admonishes the Corinthian believers. "In your thinking be adults" (1 Corinthians 14:20).

For us, too, it's advice well taken.

Trust God, and Be Brave

Years ago, a friend of mine—a deeply spiritual woman with an unquestionable commitment to God—went through a period of searching. She longed for a more fulfilling relationship with the Lord she loved, and in her seeking, she became involved with a fringe group that threatened to lead her in the wrong direction.

She was exploring, and her exploration took her on a side path that promised deeper spiritual insight but failed to deliver. It didn't take her long to find out that this was *not* what she was looking for, and she returned rather quickly to the faith that had always sustained her soul.

Some of the Christians around her condemned and shamed her for her brief expedition into the shadows at the edge of the clearing. And, certainly, the path was not the one she needed to follow. Nevertheless, the experience worked in her life to bring her to a deeper understanding of the true nature of God . . . and, in the long run, a more viable, active faith life.

In short, the Lord used it for good because her heart was seeking God.

Many of us become bitterly disappointed when the religious community, our families, or our friends denounce our search for deeper meaning rather than encourage our exploration. We often find ourselves confronted by individuals who think they know what is right for everyone, who believe that God has only one way—and that a very limited way—of leading people, of directing them into spiritual truth.

The frustrating reality is, most people opt for very soft food from a very shallow bowl. Most people avoid the conflicts and complications that inevitably accompany spiritual exploration; they'd rather stay home with their feet up, eating popcorn and handing down dogma.

So what do we do? How do we deal with these self-appointed deputies of the Spirit who truly believe they have responsibility for setting us back on the straight and narrow?

We can allow them to deter us from the journey.

Or we can trust God, and be brave.

In *Song of the Silent Harp,* a magnificent saga of the Irish potato famine and the immigration of Irish refugees to American soil, novelist B. J. Hoff paints a moving portrait of a character who faced just such a dilemma. Evan Whittaker, a stuttering, mild-mannered Englishman, encounters the greatest challenge of his mundane life when God calls him to take an enormous risk. A choice lies before him: to obey the demands of his employer, a hard-hearted landlord who is evicting the Irish peasants from their land; or to throw in his lot with the Irish and do his best to protect them.

Evan has never performed a single courageous act in his life. Unequipped for such heroism, he prays for strength . . . and answers. And, although God's direction means that he must abandon everything he has worked for, he finds peace in the decision to launch into the unknown:

He drew a deep breath, and in his own exhaled sigh, he heard his father's familiar voice: *"Trust God, and be brave."* . . . He was amazed at the peace that filled him, relieved that he seemed to know what he must do. Not *how* he was going to do it, at least not yet. But for now, it was enough to know that he must act, and that God would be with him when he did.[*]

"TRUST GOD, AND BE BRAVE"

If we intend to be spiritual explorers, to follow the unknown paths and journey into unmapped territory, we must learn to trust God. Like Christian in *The Pilgrim's Progress*, we must put our hands to our ears, shut out the voices that would call us back to safety and sameness, and run with all our might toward the woods, where Guardian waits to lead us on our way.

The voices behind us, even those friends and loved ones who think they are acting in our best interests, might well divert us from the purposes of God. The Christian community should be a place where our explorations are nurtured and encouraged, an environment of trust where we can join with others who are walking a similar path. Sometimes, however, those who love us most have difficulty entrusting us to God, or trusting God to lead us. They want to protect us, to keep us safe from possible harm, to hedge us in with a barrier of well-meaning love. But in so doing, they often stand in the way of our response to the One who calls us forward.

We need to listen to our friends, our family, and our

[*]B. J. Hoff, *Song of the Silent Harp* (Minneapolis: Bethany House Publishers, 1991), 176.

churches, to consider carefully what they have to say. We should not automatically reject their loving attempts at protection or condemn them for not seeing things our way. But in the final analysis, we need to listen to God first, and to trust God most. We need to embrace our own explorations, even when we can't please everybody, even when others are afraid we are taking the wrong path . . . even if we risk falling down the mountain and breaking an arm in the process.

And we need to be brave.

Spiritual courage is a rare and precious commodity in our world. Few people have the fearlessness to ask the difficult questions, or to live without an answer. For too many years we have put our minds on hold, avoided confrontation with our own souls, opted for predictable responses and prearranged explanations.

We need to confirm within our spirits the truth that bravery is a virtue, that God is big enough to handle our confusion and struggle, our anger and pain . . . that the One who calls us out will be with us, even if we make some mistakes along the way.

And we need to summon the fortitude to admit that sometimes the rules change.

In Acts 10, Peter resisted when God offered him unclean animals to eat.* A devout Jew, Peter scrupulously kept the Law and insisted that others do the same. Then God changed the rules . . . and Peter had to be told three times before he got the point.

Valid and appropriate restrictions for an eight-year-old aren't intended to last forever. As we make our way

*A fuller discussion of this passage appears in chapter 7, "The Open Heart."

toward adulthood, rules give way to responsibility; we learn to handle matches without singeing our fingers or burning down the house. In the spiritual realm, too, the guidelines that governed our early and formative years fall away as we grow. We learn to take custody of our own life, to listen to God for ourselves, to make decisions based not on the old regulations, but on an adult account-ability to God and to our own soul.

It takes courage to swim against the tide, to say "No thank you" to the voices that would call you back. It takes determination to climb up the mountain, to enter the dark woods and keep on going.

It takes nerve to question what you have been taught, to examine your faith, to find your own way, to make your relationship with God truly personal, a product of your own investigation and study.

It takes trust to launch out into the deep waters . . . and to allow others the freedom to do the same.

But you have been called to this journey. You are set-ting out to discover a new world, a world where faith is built on reality, where what you see and experience has meaning and purpose.

You are destined to be an explorer, and you will never be the same again.

Launch out, voyager.

Trust God.

And be brave.

CHAPTER ELEVEN

Creative Living

> At the still point of the turning world . . .
> there the dance is . . .
> Except for the point, the still point,
> There would be no dance.
> —T. S. ELIOT

It is January in Minnesota. Snow covers the ground and keeps on coming. The windchills approach forty below. And my heart is cold, cold.

I cannot write this chapter . . . this teasing, taunting chapter on creativity.

I cannot.

I have tried. And I feel like a fraud.

For days, for weeks, I have labored, struggling to find the fading spark in a creative soul that feels lifeless and barren, unproductive as the cracked, caked mud in a dry riverbed.

Two days ago I wrote a poem in my personal journal, describing my creative self as a wave frozen motionless in mid-break, "arching nowhere." I was stuck in the ice. My soul had fallen, and I couldn't get up.

Then, suddenly, my mind flashed back to an old Christmas hymn — one we rarely sing anymore:

> *In the bleak midwinter,*
> *Frosty wind made moan,*
> *Earth stood hard as iron,*
> *Water like a stone;*
> *Snow had fallen, snow on snow,*
> *Snow on snow,*
> *In the bleak midwinter,*
> *Long ago. . . .*

And I remembered . . . in the bleak midwinter, when hope was nearly gone and hearts languished on the verge of despair . . .

Jesus came.

Angels appeared.

Shepherds rejoiced.

Wise men knelt to worship.

And all history, all human life, was changed in that moment.

The story of what happened during that "bleak midwinter" is not simply the narrative of a young girl giving birth to a baby boy in a cold and dreary stable. It is the victorious triumph-song of a loving Creator who breathed the divine image into human life at Creation, and then went on to enflesh that image in the Incarnation.

It is a story of ultimate creativity . . . God with us in a way we could never have dreamed. And as part of our journey, we are called to share in the riches . . . to live in that Incarnation.

LIVING SOULS

The biblical Creation story gives us hints as to what God had in mind when the image of God was imparted to human life. "God created humankind . . . in the image of God . . . male and female," Genesis tells us. Then "the Lord God . . . breathed into his nostrils the breath of life; and man became a living soul" (Genesis 1:27, NRSV; 2:7, KJV).

The Lord didn't go to all this individual trouble of creating human life, Spirit-breathed, image-of-God life, just because the Garden of Eden needed tending and good help was hard to find. Everything else in creation had sprung spontaneously from the Word of God's mouth — God spoke, and it was, and it was good. Why, then, all this particular attention given to human beings?

I believe it was because the Incarnation was coming — the embodiment of the Christ as God in human flesh. From the very beginning, God intended that the divine image should be reflected in human life — breathed into humanity at its inception, fully revealed in the person of the Messiah. And that divine image, in my mind, is the God-given power of *creativity*.

We were, the Scriptures tell us, "created in the image of God." And God's first recorded act is the act of *creation* — the mind-boggling, unbelievably varied, infinitely intricate detailing of leaf and flower, icicle and star, beast and bird. No two snowflakes, no two fingerprints, no two fern leaves are exactly alike . . . everything, visible and invisible, bears the unmistakable mark of God's love, power, patience, and imagination. This is our legacy from the Creator — the breath of God, the spirit of creating.

Strictly speaking, of course, we do not truly create. The closest we come to actual creation is the engendering of human life, and even that begins with an egg and a sperm initially designed by God.

Creation is the generation of new life out of nothing . . . and that we cannot do. Even the most basic laws of physics teach us that matter is constant; it can combine, change forms, multiply, and divide; but it can be neither created nor destroyed. In the final analysis, only God can create.

Creativity, however, is a different matter altogether. Creativity is our part in creation, our expression of the image of the divine within us. When we express our creative gifts, we take the basic elements of creation —words, marble, canvas, paint, movement, musical notes —and rearrange them to make something new, something unique, something that has never been seen before . . . something that bears our imprint just as we bear God's image.

"But I'm not creative," you protest. "I can't write poems or sing or dance or sculpt or paint . . . or do *anything!* I'm simply not creative at all. . . ."

Yes, you are. Or at least you have the potential for it.

You can read a story that sparks the imagination of a child.

You can build a birdhouse, grow calla lilies, paint a barn, put up wallpaper, sew curtains for the den, create a masterpiece pizza, write a letter to a long-lost friend, decorate a room, reel in the great-granddaddy of all large-mouth bass, spot the first robin of the season, bake the best oatmeal cookies in the neighborhood. . . .

And then stand back, survey your handiwork, and say, "It is good."

The creative image imparted by God is not an exclusive gift for the Michelangelos and Mozarts of this world. It is for all of us who, with fear and trembling, strike out from our walled garden and take the risk to enter the woods beyond.

Somewhere along the path, we find ourselves responding to the beauty of the world around us, to the adventure that lies before us. And we want to *do* something to give expression to that response.

Whatever the medium of our creativity—words or rhythm, fabric or paint, motion or stillness—we need, somehow, to mark the moment . . . to grasp and hold and nurture the creative spirit within us . . . to become a *living soul.*

Sadly, the world around us—even the religious world— rarely encourages such nurturing. The creative arts are often met with suspicion and condemnation. We are taught, usually by implication, that God is pleased only with "spiritual" activities such as Bible study, prayer, and service. Devotion to creative pursuits is perceived as self-gratifying at best, carnal and sinful at worst.

We are surrounded by dead souls—corpses with heartbeats who go about the business of life like zombies, killing time and suffocating their own spirits in the process. We are deluged with deadening influences from society, the church, even our own families, who simply want us to fit into the accepted mold and stop causing so much trouble. We are not given the liberty to rejoice in life and explore the possibilities for our own creative ventures. We are told instead to keep quiet, to quit rocking the boat, to sit still.

Clarissa Pinkola Estes, in her best-selling book *Women*

Who Run with the Wolves, identifies this kind of deadening process as the "psychic surgery" society performs upon the creative soul:

> Children who display a strong instinctive nature often experience significant suffering in early life. . . . They are curious, artful, and have gentle eccentricities of various sorts, ones that, if developed, will constitute the basis for their creativity for the rest of their lives. . . . Creative life is the soul's food and water. . . . Unfortunately, [the child may] be subjected to her parents' attempts at psychic surgery over and over again, for they are trying to remake the child . . . trying to change what her soul requires of her. Though her soul requires seeing, the culture around her requires sightlessness. Though her soul wishes to speak its truth, she is pressured to be silent.*

Whatever our creative directions, we cannot depend upon the world around us to encourage us to embrace and nurture the creative life that is within us. We must do it for ourselves, with an awareness that it may be the most important thing we ever do.

BEING FRUITFUL

God's first command to the newly made souls in Paradise was "Be fruitful" (Genesis 1:28). Certainly, the command referred partly to the need for procreating the species. But the implication goes far beyond physical

*Clarissa Pinkola Estes, *Women Who Run with the Wolves* (New York: Ballantine Books, 1992), 173.

reproduction. Adam and Eve had creative work to do —
pruning, digging, fertilizing, harvesting . . . and the
most intriguing of their duties, naming the thousands of
species God had created. God made the animals; Adam
named them. And in the naming, human beings became
a part of the creative process.

Right here, in chapters 1 and 2 of the Bible, we see
God's emphasis on creativity . . . the prime directive for
the revelation of the divine image. Madeleine L'Engle, in
Walking on Water, comments:

> God asked Adam to name all the animals, which was
> asking Adam to help in the creation of their whole-
> ness. When we name each other, we are sharing in
> the joy and privilege of incarnation.*

As we leave behind our walled garden and take the
risk of journeying into the unknown, we need to be
aware of the importance of that creative gift: of cultivat-
ing it, nurturing it, giving it room to grow and flourish,
so it too will be fruitful and multiply. No matter how the
world around us may try to stifle and stultify our creative efforts, no matter if our own early training has
tried to root it out of us, we must nevertheless find a
way to give ourselves fully to the developing of God's
image within us.

The image of God has been with us, in us, from the
beginning . . . the breath, the life, the creativity given in
love by One who has called us to share in creation. Yet

*Madeleine L'Engle, *Walking on Water* (Wheaton, Ill.: Harold Shaw Publishers,
1980), 46.

throughout history we have denied it, ignored it, allowed it to calcify within us, or sought to claim it for ourselves.

We do not see the creative gift for what it is . . .

God with us.

Occasionally we have glimpses — the snatches of an unwritten song that play over and over in our mind; the idea that awakens us in the middle of the night; the turn of phrase that captures our imaginations and will not let go. God is with us, prodding us to go up and out, beyond our mundane routines, to give ourselves heart and soul to the birthing of the image of the divine within us. As Madeleine L'Engle says,

> To paint a picture or to write a story or to compose a song is an incarnational activity. The artist is a servant who is willing to be a birthgiver. In a very real sense the artist (male or female) should be like Mary who, when the angel told her that she was to bear the Messiah, was obedient to the command. . . .
>
> I believe that each work of art, whether it is a work of great genius or something very small, comes to the artist and says, "Here I am. Enflesh me. Give birth to me." And the artist either says, "My soul doth magnify the Lord," and willingly becomes the bearer of the work, or refuses.[*]

We give birth to something new: a song, a dance, a poem, a recipe, a fishing lure, a note in a child's lunch box. These are the spiritual offspring of our creativity,

[*]L'Engle, *Walking on Water,* 18.

the children of our imagination, who need nurture and love and validation and ongoing care. Just as we do with our own flesh-and-blood sons and daughters, we name them, giving them a title, a description . . . an identification: "I made this." And whether we realize the source or not, we are bringing forth the image of God—the individuality woven into the fabric of our soul.

SEEING

God's second command to Adam and Eve in the Garden was "See!" (Genesis 1:29, NRSV). *Look around you,* God said. *See what I have given you . . . observe all that I have created . . . keep your eyes open . . . appreciate the variety . . . be aware of what I have done. . . .*

And the injunction is the same for us today, for we are called to share in the creative image that God has given us: *Be fruitful; be aware.*

See.

In my generation, when children were beginning to read, one of the first words they learned was *see.*

See Jane run. Run, run, run. Look, Jane, look!

Creativity, the expression of God's image within us, is more than a matter of *doing,* of *producing.* It is a way of *seeing.*

Seeing—truly seeing, with heart and soul as well as brain and retina—can be at once a stimulus to human creativity and an expression of God's creative image. I can stand for half an hour and watch the wind rippling across the lake, noting the patterns made by the breeze and the still deep pools beneath the tree branches, rejoicing in the sheer beauty and freedom of the moment.

That experience *may* stimulate some tangible expression of my creative spirit — a sketch, perhaps; a description in my journal; an image to share with my Wednesday night discovery group. But in and of itself, entirely apart from any further imaginative usefulness, the moment can be an act of creativity. If I see it — truly see it, take it into my heart, and allow it to work within me to gentle me, ennoble me, and draw me closer to the Creator — the experience of seeing alone is worthwhile.

Annie Dillard, Pulitzer prize–winning author of *Pilgrim at Tinker Creek,* has a unique understanding of imaginative sight, founded in an awareness of God's creativity:

> I see something, some event that would otherwise have been utterly missed and lost; or something sees me, some enormous power brushes me with its clean wing, and I resound like a beaten bell. . . .
>
> Seeing is of course very much a matter of verbalization. Unless I call my attention to what passes before my eyes, I simply won't see it.*

Dillard goes on to give an awe-inspiring example of this kind of spiritual sight, a description of seeing a cedar tree silhouetted in a sunset:

> I was walking along Tinker Creek thinking of nothing at all and I saw the tree with the lights in it. . . . I stood on the grass with the lights in it,

*Annie Dillard, *Pilgrim at Tinker Creek* (New York: Harper and Row, 1974), 12, 30.

grass that was wholly fire, utterly focused and
utterly dreamed. It was less like seeing than like
being for the first time seen, knocked breathless by
a powerful glance. The flood of fire abated, but I'm
still spending the power. Gradually the lights went
out in the cedar, the colors died, the cells unflamed
and disappeared. I was still ringing. I had been my
whole life a bell, and never knew it until at that
moment I was lifted and struck.[*]

My father is a person with that kind of spiritual sight.
Not the pious, in-your-face kind of religion that masquerades as spirituality and says, "Well, look here, this is the
spiritual significance of this moment—see it?" Rather, he
sees things, and takes them in: the humor in a moment of
embarrassment, the peace of a glassy lake at dawn, the
beauty in the delicacy of a flower. During his retirement
years, he has learned to express that vision in stained
glass—beautiful, handcrafted works he presents as gifts
to his family and friends. At other times in his life, he has
expressed that same creativity in his career, in his fishing
prowess, in his storytelling. But the vision is the same. He
sees beyond the surface, embraces the spiritual truth of
life, and in the process finds joy in the journey.

Created in the image of God, we are called to venture
forth with our eyes open and our heart ready to respond.
We may not have the talent to write the next great American novel, astound the world with an oratorio, or sculpt a
timeless statue from a slab of marble. But we dare not

[*]Ibid., 33–34.

deny or ignore the creative spirit God has placed within us—the ability to see, and to be fruitful.

"Do not be conformed to this world," the apostle Paul wrote (Romans 12:2, NRSV). Don't let yourself be squeezed into a mold, deadened in spirit by those around you who do not recognize and cannot nurture the creative image of God within you.

Look around.

See the wonders of the world.

Embrace your adventure.

Respond to the risk.

Cherish this child of your heart, this image of the Creator that has been birthed through your creativity.

You are being led for a purpose. . . .

The breath of life is in you to become a living soul.

CHAPTER TWELVE

Resting in the High Country

The sudden illumination—
We had the experience, but missed the meaning,
And approach to the meaning restores the experience
In a different form, beyond any meaning
We can assign to happiness.
　—T. S. ELIOT

If I've heard it once, I've heard it a hundred times. My longtime friend, who has been my personal and professional colleague for fifteen years, looks at me with a wistful, faraway expression and says, "You're living the dream you've always had, aren't you?"

In a way, she is right.

Since I was four, I dreamed of being a writer. At that age, of course, I had no idea what the process would involve. I simply knew I was fascinated with words, the way they worked magic on the page and in the mind . . . and I wanted to do that.

Now I'm doing it. It's turned out to be quite different from what I had imagined, I must admit, but it is a delightful, stimulating process . . . most of the time.

I am living the dream; not only my dream, but the dream many people would love to have. I have established my own business and work out of my home—a huge Victorian house built in 1889, with interesting nooks and crannies, stained-glass windows, and open oak staircases. I couldn't ask for a more creative setting.

In other ways, too, I am living my dream. Over the past few years I have come through some difficult personal issues and found a place of peace. I am going deeper in my spiritual life. I am at home with myself, and with God.

For a little while, I have been resting in the high country . . . in the upper reaches, where the air is clear and clean, where life seems simpler, more basic. For now, I rejoice in the clarity of vision, in the strength of the Presence, in the radiance of the moment. I will never forget these days of living the dream.

For now, I will exult in the wonder.

But not forever. . . .

TRANSFORMATION MOUNTAIN

High on a mountainside, away from the demands of the crowd and the incessant clamor of voices, three men stood gaping in awe at the miraculous transformation taking place. Their eyes squinting against the intensity of the light, their skin warmed by divine heat, they watched in amazement as Jesus was transfigured before them, revealed in utter majesty and power.*

It was a moment like no other. On that rocky preci-

*The story of the Transfiguration is told in Matthew 17:1-8, Mark 9:2-9, and Luke 9:28-36.

pice, heaven and earth met and joined; transcendency merged with temporal reality. And the disciples who were present—Peter, James, and John—were given a unique glimpse of the glory of the Godhead.

Sometimes it happens for us, too.

Occasionally—usually when we least expect it—we are led up to a high place, apart from the stress and trouble of the world below. The path may be steep and the ascent dangerous and taxing. Along the way, we may complain that the road is too hard. But when we get to the top and the clouds open before us, we find ourselves imbued with a transforming joy. We understand who we are in the presence of the Almighty, and everything seems to make sense for the first time.

It is a moment of divine stillness, of spiritual oneness, of supernatural understanding.

It is a gift.

And then, like Peter, we begin to expect that we can stay forever.

We stake out the territory, mark out the foundation for our spiritual cabin in the high country. We plan a picture window overlooking the site of glory. We put in a fireplace to capture the holy flame. We're determined not to let the miracle escape this time.

But it does escape.

The miracle is for the moment; it knocks us off our feet and then is gone before we can right ourselves. It stuns us with sensation and then leaves us wondering if it really happened at all.

It happened, all right.

But like the swift flash of a hawk's wing as it darts into

the stream after a trout, or the ladder-shaft of light reaching up to heaven from a cloud-banked sunset, the miracle is elusive. It is not given to us on tape, for replaying again and again on the VCR like a favorite scene. As Annie Dillard observed of the "grace wholly gratuitous" in nature, it's "one show to a customer." *

Our moments on the heights with God, certainly, are experiences of pristine joy. We are led up the Mount of Transfiguration; we are startled and overwhelmed and changed forever by our glimpse of the unshrouding of the Holy One.

But we cannot stay.

Even as the glory fades from our astonished eyes, we see the hand pointing us back down the mountainside, back to the valley.

Back to reality.

And to us, as to Peter, Jesus says: *Enjoy this moment . . . be inspired; be stimulated; be transformed. The high country offers a glorious respite, but this is not a permanent residence. Don't build your house here.*

HOLY RESTLESSNESS

Two men set out with their families on a journey.

Abraham received a call from God to leave his country and his people and venture out into the unknown, to a land God would give him.

Lot, Abraham's nephew, went along for the ride. *

After a while, however, Lot tired of the ceaseless travel-

---

*Annie Dillard, *Pilgrim at Tinker Creek* (New York: Harper & Row, 1974), 7, 16.

*The story of Abraham and Lot is told in Genesis 12–19.

ing. He wanted a permanent residence, a place to settle down. So, with his household, he chose a spot that provided him with comfort and security—the city of Sodom.

Before long, Lot was "sitting in the gateway" of Sodom (Genesis 19:1)—occupying a place of prominence among the people destined for destruction. He was established, successful . . . and in grave danger.

Abraham, meanwhile, continued to journey. God showed him the land that was to be his, with the accompanying command: "Go, walk through the length and breadth of the land, for I am giving it to you" (Genesis 13:17).

Abraham, the father of faith, did not accept the luxury of sitting down and contemplating all he had achieved. "Walk on," God told him. "Keep going. There is much you have not seen."

Surely Abraham had his own holy mountains—the places where God met him in glory and revealed the divine nature to him. But he did not ask to pitch his tent there. He was blessed with a holy restlessness, the desire to go deeper, to discover more, to explore the land that God had promised him.

Years later, when the reins of Israelite command passed from Moses to Joshua, the Lord reiterated the call to come down from the mountain, to walk through the land. To Joshua, God made the command even more explicit: "I will give you every place where you set your foot" (Joshua 1:3).

It is all too easy for us to give in to the desire to stay where we are, especially when where we are is a place of spiritual revelation and peace and fulfillment. We long to capture the mystery, to hold onto the moment of transfiguration, to bask forever in the glory.

But we cannot.

God has called us to walk through the land, to come down from the mountain and continue the journey. We take the glory with us when we go, but go we must . . . even if we'd rather stay on the heights.

Metaphysical poet George Herbert understood the place and purpose of holy restlessness in our lives. In his poem "The Pulley," Herbert postulates that at Creation, God poured out on humankind the abundance of divine blessings . . . all blessings except one—*rest*. In the poem, God explains the decision to hold back the gift of rest:

> *For if I should (said he)*
> *Bestow this jewell also on my creature,*
> *He would adore my gifts in stead of me,*
> *And rest in Nature, not the God of Nature. . . .*
>
> *Yet let him keep the rest,*
> *But keep them with repining restlesnesse:*
> *Let him be rich and wearie, that at least*
> *If goodness leade him not, yet wearinesse*
> *May tosse him to my breast.*[*]

Whether we realize it or not, we are called to a measure of restlessness . . . that divine withholding that acts as a pulley to draw our heart to God. We are destined to explore, to survey the land, to strike out for the

[*]George Herbert, "The Pulley," in *The Complete Poems of George Herbert* (Oxford: Oxford University Press, 1941), 160. The original spellings have been retained for authenticity.

horizon. The restlessness is given by God as motivation to keep us from building a permanent residence on the heights.

Sometimes, however, we misunderstand the restlessness and interpret it as a sign of discontent, even of rebellion. We think—or have been taught—that once we have seen the glory on the mountain, we are destined to live there. And so we try to still that longing in our heart, to put a lid on the desire to learn more about ourselves and God. We attempt to quiet the yearning, to muffle the Voice that urges us, *Come out.*

Or we mistake peace for complacency and lose sight of the fact that we are called to "walk." When we are granted a time of rest and peace so that our soul may be restored, we get a glimpse of the beauty and wonder of the place . . . and then we begin to think that we can call a permanent halt at that place in our spiritual journey. We want to put down roots, take up residence, and establish ourselves in the city gates.

We get comfortable.

We think we can claim for our own what we see with our eyes or imagine with our mind, rather than the ground we actually set foot upon.

We try desperately to ignore the Voice that whispers to us in the night.

But to us—as to Abraham, as to Quester in our parable, as to Peter on the Mount of Transfiguration—the call continues to resound: *Don't build your house here. Descend from the mountain; walk through the length and breadth of this land. Come out; there is much you have not seen.*

ARRIVALS AND DEPARTURES

Recently I drove to Minneapolis to meet my business partner at the airport. Abandoning me to blowing snow and windchills of thirty below, she had gone blithely off to teach at a conference in central Florida. After five days in the balmy breezes and temperate climates, she was coming back. And now the windchill was *forty* below. Poetic justice.

As I waited for the plane to land, checking the monitors to make sure I was at the right gate, I noticed something that puzzled me—there were far more *outgoing* flights listed than *incoming* ones . . . almost three to one.

And I wondered: Is that the way life is? Are we always moving on, taking a new departure, seeking a new destination? Do the outbound flights always outnumber the incoming ones?

Maybe they do. Maybe that is the way it is supposed to be.

There are, of course, places of arrival that are intended to be more or less permanent in our life: marriage, family responsibilities, spiritual commitments. When we say "I do," we mean it to last a lifetime. When we bring a new life into the world, we accept the obligation for many years of care and development. When we give ourselves over to God's purposes, we expect that it will be forever . . . and beyond.

Yet even the "permanent" places of our life are themselves launching pads, springboards to new experiences and new directions; ever-deepening understanding of ourselves, of God, and of others. Anyone who has been married knows that a lifetime commitment to another person inevitably leads to change — positive change, we hope — spiritual growth, a stronger love, a more significant bond. Anyone who has raised a child finds out all too quickly that flexibility is the order of the day, that maturing must occur in the parent as well as in the child.

So it is in our spiritual life. Those places of peace and rest, of glory and fulfillment and contentment, are not intended to make us complacent but to stir us to a deeper level of trust, to greater challenge. We are called to walk through the land, to set one foot at a time upon the ground we intend to occupy. The outbound flights are always leaving.

Departing, of course, does not mean that we necessarily leave behind us what God has given in the past. We don't forsake our home and family responsibilities to launch out into new spiritual waters. We don't change spouses when the restlessness comes upon us, or automatically sell our homes or take another job in an unfamiliar city.

More important than the exterior changes are the interior transformations, the deep inner workings that we are called to. Our *soul* needs to be outward bound, moving beyond what we know and understand to explore new territory. Our *heart* should be searching for insight along the way.

Sometimes, like Lot, we dig our heels in and refuse to move. This may not be the best of what spiritual life has to offer, but it's pretty comfortable. We know the ropes. We've just about gotten it figured out. And we'd rather stay put, thank you.

What Lot didn't realize—and what we often forget—is that staying put can be dangerous. God was moving on. Destruction was coming. And Lot was sunning himself at the city gates, oblivious to the need to get himself in motion.

If we're serious about going deeper in our inner life, we need to remember that the spiritual journey is just that—a *journey*. It's not a circular speed track, nor is it a direct flight to a specified destination. It's a voyage of discovery, and we don't discover anything new by settling on our haunches and putting another log on the fire. We claim the uncharted territory by putting our feet on the ground and walking the length and breadth of the land.

A TIME OF HOLY REST

When Peter and the other disciples were on the mount with Jesus, God spoke an important word to them—a truth that almost gets overlooked in the flash and fire of the transforming miracle. God said, "This is my Son. . . . Listen to him!" (Mark 9:7).

Christ was the one who led them into the high places.

Christ was the one who pointed them downward, into the valley.

The moment of glory was God's idea. So was the return to reality.

There is a time for ascending the mountain, into the stillness and the majesty, away from the clamor of life as we know it. There is a time for spiritual retreat, for basking in the glow of God's presence and forgetting everything around us.

These are magnificent times, moments resplendent with grace . . . days and hours of wonder and awe.

If you are presently on the mountain, at a place in your spiritual journey where you feel content and fulfilled, rejoice and be thankful. God orchestrates these seasons of peace, these times of security and contentment. There is a time for processing what we have learned, for allowing the new wonders of our life on the journey to sink in and become part of us. There is a time for resting on the heights.

The problem is, we sometimes misinterpret what rest really is, what contentment is designed to be.

In his famous poem "The Lotos-Eaters," Tennyson recounts the Homeric episode of Odysseus and his men arriving at an island overflowing with a sweet and seductive fruit. The sailors—fearless men whose lives were built on adventure and conquest—eat the lotos fruit and suddenly lose the will to continue on their quest. "Our island home/Is far beyond the wave," they say. "We will no longer roam."

Lulled into complacency by the effects of the lotos fruit, the warriors give up the idea of launching out again. Even the memories of their wives and families back home cannot motivate them to leave the island and brave the dangers of the sea:

> *We have had enough of action, and of motion. . . .*
> *Surely, surely slumber is more sweet than toil, the shore*
> *Than labor in the deep mid-ocean, wind and wave and oar;*
> *O, rest ye, brother mariners, we will not wander more.**

*Alfred, Lord Tennyson, "The Lotos-Eaters," in *The Norton Anthology of English Literature*, Vol. 2, 4th Edition (New York: W. W. Norton, Inc., 1979), 1104–1108.

Sometimes, in the moment of glory, we can forget that our prime directive is ongoing discovery—of God, of ourselves, of what it means to be conformed to the image of Christ. The lure of complacency works upon our soul like the fruit of the lotos flower, drugging us into a false sense of well-being, making us believe that we have done all that we can do, gone as far as we can go. We want to build a permanent house upon the mountain.

But the rest that God offers holds no such lethargy; it is, in fact, an integral part of the movement of our soul up to higher truth, into deeper insight. God gives us rest *along the way.*

To Moses, called to lead the Israelites through the wilderness into the Promised Land, the Lord said, "My Presence will go with you, and I will give you rest" (Exodus 33:14).

God did not instruct Moses to stay where he was, but to continue onward. The *rest* came not through inactivity or complacency, but through an awareness of God's presence on the journey.

Similarly, through the prophet Jeremiah, God gives us insight into the nature of the rest the Lord has promised to those who follow:

"Stand at the crossroads, and look, and ask for the ancient paths, where the good way lies; and walk in it, and find rest for your souls" (Jeremiah 6:16, NRSV).

Certainly, we find an inner satisfaction, a peace, in responding to the call to come out and venture into new spiritual territory. But that rest is not a deadening, enervating force that causes us to stop in our tracks and refuse to go further. It is a spiritual harmony that comes with progress, a clarity of mind and heart that accompanies the deepening of our soul.

Peace comes in the midst of the adventure, not at the end of the road.

Rest is the result of walking in the way set before us.

We can be at peace and still feel that holy restlessness. We can treasure the mountaintop experience even as we prepare for the descent. We can long to go further without abandoning everything we have gained. Fulfillment doesn't stop us from moving forward — it can, in fact, motivate us to go on.

But if we find ourselves longing to stay where we are, to capture the miracle in stasis and not have to change anymore, we may be on dangerous ground.

For change will occur . . . transition is inevitable.

Like it or not, the time will come to pull up the tent stakes and strike out into the wilderness again. The One who called us to follow up the mountainside will point us down to the valley once more. For the Voice that called us from the safety of our walled gardens keeps on calling: *Come out; there is much you have not seen.*

Relish the restful times, the days of transfiguration, the sweet untroubled moments of serenity, the blessed nights of placid peace.

Give thanks for the respite, for the chance to light a fire and warm your bones.

Rejoice in the lingering season of tranquility, when a hallowed calm hovers over your soul.

But do not try to build a permanent dwelling in the high country.

Resist the fruit of the tempting lotos flower.

Do not give in to lethargy.

Keep your wits about you, and your senses sharp.

The holy restlessness is stirring. Soon it will be time to rise up, throw your cloak about your shoulders, and walk on.

PART FIVE

The Valley of Decision

After a while, Quester's initial passion over the book Guardian had given her began to subside. They struck out again, walking endlessly through dark forests and bright meadows.

And gradually, Quester came to recognize a different emotion rising up in her heart. She loved being with Guardian, of course, and exploring the world at his side. But she was disturbed, as well. She didn't tell him, but for all her happiness, she secretly wondered if he truly knew where they were headed.

She had been brought up to live a purposeful existence — accomplishing something, having a goal, a mission, a point of arrival. She and Guardian didn't seem to be getting anywhere; they seemed simply to be going.

Then one afternoon her fears were confirmed. They had reentered the forest and were following a rocky path when they came to a fork in the road.

"Which way do we go, Guardian?" Quester asked.

"Which way do you want to go?"

"You want *me* to decide which path to take?"

"Yes. Which way do we go?"

Quester paused, confused. Guardian was supposed to be leading her to—well, to wherever they were going. Shouldn't *he* make the choice?

"Which is the right way?" she asked finally.

"The one that is not left," he quipped, and his shadowed eyes smiled.

"Don't give me riddles, Guardian!" Quester snapped. "There are two paths: one is right, and the other is wrong. Now, which is the right way for us to go?"

"To go where?"

"Wherever it is we're going!" Quester frowned. "The paths go opposite directions. Which one takes us toward our destination?"

"Either," Guardian said simply.

"How can that be? They cannot possibly end up at the same place!"

"Nor can we," Guardian replied. "But either road we take will bring us to where we are supposed to be."

Quester glared at him and turned on her heel, striking off down the path to the left. Guardian drew his cloak around him and followed at his same steady, unhurried pace.

CHAPTER THIRTEEN

Nagging Doubts

If you came this way,
Taking any route, starting from anywhere,
At any time or at any season,
It would always be the same: You would have to put off
Sense and notion.
    —T. S. ELIOT

Like millions of other Americans this week, I have spent my evenings watching the winter Olympics. The action—skating, skiing, luge, bobsled—is exciting, and like everyone else, I cry when the flags are raised and the national anthems are played at the medal ceremonies.

But even more interesting to me are the behind-the-scenes tales—the stories of how the athletes got to the Olympics in the first place. This year, a mogul skier has come back from a devastating knee injury to ski for the gold. Another athlete, a three-time Olympian, his speed-skating career marred by failure and personal tragedy, has only one chance left to take home a medal. It's now or never. Do or die. The pressure is on.

In a heartbreaking turn of events, a downhill racer loses his one opportunity to compete when his ski binding breaks as he comes out of the gate. Despairing, he lashes out at the snow with his ski pole, but he cannot change his fate. He trudges back up the hill and disappears—perhaps to train again for the next opportunity . . . perhaps to give it up forever.

From all over the world they come. This is their moment on the mountaintop. For two weeks, or a few seconds, they are standing on the heights.

Then reality hits—in a broken ski binding or ice on a blade or a minute overcompensation on the luge track—and their dreams crash in around them.

I watch the ones who lose, and wonder: *Was it worth it? Do they doubt the wisdom of following the Olympic dream, of giving up the security of anonymity for the slim possibility of a single moment of glory?*

We who journey in spiritual realms are like those Olympic athletes. We leave the security of the walled garden behind, launch out, take a tremendous risk to explore the potential of our life with God. Occasionally we are led up to the heights, onto the mountain where the clouds part and we glimpse a transforming moment of majesty.

Then we are called down the mountainside again . . . back to the everyday journey, where the storms drench us and the stones along the path bruise our feet and make us weep.

The fleeting radiance was real, certainly. We remember it, turning it over in our mind, recalling the images, trying to hold on to the feelings we had at the time.

But the glory fades, and we begin to doubt:

Have I come all this way for nothing?
Is anyone out there?
Where do I go from here?

THE COURAGE OF HONEST DOUBT

Usually the church won't tell you; seldom will your friends admit it . . . but honest doubt can prove to be one of your greatest allies in the quest for a deeper spiritual life. Doubt can cause us to question, to delve beyond the surface of things, to risk looking stupid for the sake of drawing closer to God. Doubt can purify faith, stripping away the superficialities and carving the soul down to its streamlined core, to the issues that are really important. Doubt can be a refining fire.

But doubt has gotten a bad rap among religious types.

People are uncomfortable with doubt. It raises unanswered — and unanswerable — questions. It challenges the status quo. It makes us all think.

And usually we'd rather just avoid the hard stuff.

So, because of what we have been taught, doubt sometimes tangles us up. When we have doubts, we generally end up feeling guilty about the fact that we are doubting, and our genuine inquiry gets lost in a muddle of self-defeating feelings. Instead of probing further, we try to stifle our doubts. We latch on to a tight-lipped, closed-mouth version of faith, and let the questions ride.

The Bible has a few things to say about doubt, passages that are often used as cudgels to bludgeon the hearts and minds of those who question.

When Peter was walking on the water and began to

sink, Jesus said to him, "You of little faith, why did you doubt?" (Matthew 14:31).

When Christ was teaching the disciples about faith, he said, "If you have faith and do not doubt . . . you can say to this mountain, 'Go, throw yourself into the sea,' and it will be done" (Matthew 21:21).

When Jesus appeared to the disciples after the Resurrection and they were frightened, thinking they had seen a ghost, he said, "Why are you troubled, and why do doubts rise in your minds?" (Luke 24:38).

And the most oft-quoted passage of all: When Thomas refused to accept the disciples' word that Christ was risen until he put his own hand into the wounds, Jesus said, "Put your finger here; see my hands. Reach out your hand and put it into my side. Stop doubting and believe" (John 20:27).

Sadly, we have taken such Scriptures—examples of the humanity of the disciples—and, with a little help from the church, made legalistic proclamations out of them: *Stop doubting, and believe. Have faith, and do not doubt.* And then we use them to berate ourselves: *O me of little faith . . . why can't I believe perfectly, without question?*

But the context of these same passages shows no such condemning attitude. When Peter began to sink, Jesus reached out a hand to him. When the disciples couldn't fathom the reality of the Resurrection, the Lord reassured them, invited them to touch him, and even ate a fish to demonstrate that he was, indeed, alive. When Thomas came before him, Jesus exposed his hands and side and offered Thomas the opportunity to see and feel for himself.

Jude 1:22 says, "Be merciful to those who doubt."

God does not condemn us for questioning or turn an angry face away from our longing to discover the truth. To us, as to Thomas, the Savior reveals his wounds and says, "Come, touch me. Have your faith renewed."

God is merciful to those who doubt.

We need to extend the same mercy to others . . . and to ourselves.

Peter wanted to get to Christ so much that he took an enormous chance. He risked his very life to try to walk upon the water, held up only by the word of his Master. When he began to sink, Christ didn't let him drown . . . he reached out, touched him, drew him up to the surface . . . and into the embrace of the Lord he loved.

Thomas found the courage to be honest, to express what the other disciples dared not say. He revealed his heart, no matter what the cost. And Jesus responded to his tenacity by inviting him to draw close. Whether Thomas actually touched the Savior's wounds, we do not know. But in spiritual terms, certainly, he touched Jesus, and his love and faith were deepened.

Honest doubt is not for the fainthearted. It is easier, safer to keep your questions to yourself and pretend to be spiritual and full of faith. But those who dare to doubt come away from the encounter with their faith strengthened . . . and with the touch of God upon them.

SORTING THROUGH THE STRUGGLES

Most of us can identify with Quester in the parable. Things are going well; we have been on the mountaintop, caught a glimpse of glory, felt the wonder and peace of life above the crowd. We'd love to stay for a while . . . maybe forever.

But the journey goes on. And as the glory fades, we begin to wonder if the One who leads us really knows where we are going. We don't seem to be making much progress; our route seems circular, rather than a well-defined straight line toward a well-established destination.

And we begin to doubt.

We doubt ourselves: *Did I just imagine the peace, the joy, the splendor of the time of rest? Did I make it all up? Where is that glory now?*

And weren't we headed south before? I'm turned around; this feels like north. I thought I was getting the hang of this exploration stuff. . . .

What's wrong with me?

If we can be this honest, we may also doubt the motives or the wisdom of the One who leads us on:

Does Guardian have any idea where we're going? Where's that map—I want to have a look for myself. Is this rough trail really necessary? I thought I saw a wider, smoother one a mile or so back. Didn't we just pass that same tree two hours ago?

Maybe . . . maybe Guardian is deliberately leading me around in circles to see how long I'll put up with this nonsense. Maybe this is some kind of test. Or maybe he wants to confuse me. Maybe he's not so loving after all. . . .

Can I really trust the One who is supposed to be leading me?

I certainly could do better than this. Maybe I should just strike out on my own. . . .

We do have a problem with doubt.

We doubt ourselves . . . our capacity for faith, our ability to follow, sometimes even the quality and strength of our love. We wonder if we've made the right choice to put ourselves at risk in the first place. Some days we just want to go back where it's safe and the questions are all answered neatly and efficiently . . . even if the answers don't always work.

We doubt God, too . . . we aren't sure whether the divine plan is such a good idea. We want to understand, and when understanding is withheld from us, we start to wonder if even God knows the outcome of the path we are on. To our way of thinking, life was a lot better back on the Mount of Glory—or even further back, in the security of the walled garden.

But we don't say these things. It's heresy—isn't it?—to question God. It's unspiritual to get angry, to lash out at God, to demand some explanations.

We keep it all inside.

We play out the scene like good little Christians, plastering on a phony smile and murmuring, "Yes, Lord, I trust you," when all the while our mind screams silently, *What in the world is going on?*

As if God didn't know what we *really* feel.

We have a problem with doubt, all right. But the problem isn't the doubt.

The problem is, we aren't honest enough to express our doubts frankly to the God who knows all about them anyway. We don't come forward with the truth, as Thomas did. We try to suppress our questions, our uncertainties, our anger, our concerns.

In the bluntest of terms, we lie to God . . . and to our-selves.

But an enduring relationship cannot be founded on lies.

As in a marriage, a parent/child relationship, a close friendship, a business partnership, honesty is the corner-stone of lasting trust.

And honesty hurts sometimes.

It's hard.

It brings us face-to-face with our own weakness and vulnerability.

It seems easier for a wife to deceive herself and try to pretend her husband's negligence doesn't hurt her. It's initially less painful for a child to continue trying to please a demanding parent rather than face the consequences of confronting the root problem. It's simpler in the short run to ignore a betrayal rather than risk losing a friend.

It's infinitely less threatening to avoid being honest with God about the doubts and fears and uncertainties that plague us.

We are conditioned to evade the issue. We are taught to pretend, to put up a front, to act spiritual, to keep still.

But the charade is exhausting.

And real love demands more than pretense.

Real love compels us to speak what is on our mind; to ask, as Thomas did, for verification of what we have been told. Real love requires openness, exposure of the pain and doubt as well as the adoration and acceptance. Real love constrains us to step out onto the waves like Peter, to risk looking foolish or faithless in order to come to a deeper level of trust . . . in order to draw closer to the One who called us out.

When you have descended from the place of glory,
doubts may arise and darkness may cloud your vision.

But take heart. Nothing is hidden from the sight of
God.

You can be truthful; you will not shock the Lord.

Our God is big enough to handle your anger and fear.
The Lord is merciful with those who doubt, for they are
the ones who are seeking.

Love breaks forth in the presence of honesty.

Reach out with your questions and doubts.

Ask. Search. Inquire.

The wounds of love are held out before you. Let your
heart be open, and your spirit unafraid.

Come, touch the hands that bled for you. Draw near to
the wounded side.

Embrace your doubts, and have your faith renewed.

CHAPTER FOURTEEN

Who's in Charge Here?

You are not here to verify,
Instruct yourself, or inform curiosity
Or carry report. You are here to kneel
Where prayer has been valid.
　　—T. S. ELIOT

I talked to a friend this morning—a gifted, intelligent man who has been without employment for nearly a year and a half. He had just completed the first week of his new job, and he was on top of the world.

"It's wonderful," he said. "The people here are just terrific; I fit right in. And I have discovered that my mind still works . . . I feel as if I'm right in the center of God's will."

I was delighted, of course, to see him so happy and fulfilled. I rejoiced with him in his new position and the affirmation of his colleagues. But I wondered if he felt himself in the center of God's will through the dark days of restlessness when he didn't think he'd ever find the right job, during the nights of anxiety when he wondered how he'd make his house payment.

Yes, God is with him in this fresh adventure.

But was God also there when he couldn't see the light? Did God know how much pain he was in?

Did God care?

Couldn't the Lord have done something sooner?

Who's in charge here, anyway?

THE CONTROL/AUTONOMY PREDICAMENT

The question of God's control over the events of the universe—and of our individual life—has baffled believers for centuries. If God is God—omnipotent, omniscient, omnipresent—does that mean that everything that happens to me occurs according to a predetermined plan?

Some Christians would say so.

Some people believe that God's will is carved in granite, like the Ten Commandments Moses brought down from the mountain on tablets of stone. According to this perception, God orders everything in an individual's life—success or failure, health or infirmity, good times or bad—for the accomplishment of the divine will.

Others take the position that although God is all-powerful, the Spirit does not impose the will of God upon us. We are free to choose our own way and to live with our own consequences. This means, of course, that we can choose to rebel or disobey, and thus bring judgment down upon our head.

It's a difficult predicament.

If God controls our every action, jerking us around like marionettes, we don't have to take any responsibility for our decisions, but we also do not have any real free-

dom. It's all a sham, an elaborate game where the outcome is already decided.

If God *doesn't* control us, we are faced with a different
problem. We must live in constant fear of doing the
wrong thing, of making the wrong choices. We alone are
responsible for our fate, and knowing human nature, we
will probably screw up and burn in hell for all eternity.

It's the old, old dictator/watchmaker dichotomy. The
dictator image of God, carried to its logical extreme,
leaves us with a deity whose "divine plan" includes crib
death, cancer, disease, war, and countless millions of
people who suffer and die needlessly because of circumstances beyond their control. We serve a Master who is
the creator of evil as well as good, and not one we'd feel
very inclined to worship and adore.

If we subscribe to the watchmaker theory, we end up
with a benevolent but impotent supreme being who set
the world in motion and then just sat back to watch what
would happen. This spectator God is the ultimate sideline
coach, dispensing advice that nobody ever takes, power-
less or unwilling to intervene on our behalf. We may have
warm, fuzzy feelings about this grandfather God, but on
the whole such a deity seems pretty ineffective in our life.

It's not a pretty picture, is it?

Either way, we lose.

But maybe there's a different way to answer the question, Who's in charge here?

THE LOVE FACTOR

I'll admit for the record that my dictator/watch-
maker image is a simplistic one, based on the ordinary

Christian's conflicting perceptions, and not likely to satisfy the Sadducees among us. The theological debate on this issue of God's control in our life is an ongoing, never-ending dispute . . . and one I prefer not to get involved in.

But we're not here to establish theological verities. We are here to journey with God into the unknown, to find practical, workable perspectives that will help us deepen and broaden our understanding of the One who called us out.

We will never solve this dilemma.

But we can find a place of peace.

So . . . what is the answer? Is God in control, or are we free moral agents?

Yes, to both questions.

If we believe that God is God, that God has actual power and the willingness to intervene in our life, we must admit that God is in control. We pray because we expect God to respond in some significant way. We read the Scriptures because we believe that God has the right to direct us into thinking or behaving in a certain manner. We adhere to particular moral standards, even when they seem difficult, because somehow, deep inside, we know we cannot be our own final authority.

But we also know that we are not robots, automatons with preprogrammed menus of thought and behavior patterns. We have a mind and heart . . . the ability to make decisions, choices based on sound reasoning and spiritual truth. We have to grow into this autonomy, certainly, as we mature and take fuller accountability for our life. But ultimately we are responsible for ourselves in relationship to God.

And God is with us in the decision making.

When we consider the difficult dichotomy of control versus autonomy, we need to factor in one all-important issue: *love.*

Love is the variable that makes the difference in our perception of God. Neither the dictator nor the watch-maker is an image of loving involvement. The dictator dominates us; the watchmaker ignores us. The Scriptures depict God as a parent to us, but not as an abusive, manipulative parent . . . or as a negligent, abandoning one.

We have not all *been* parents, but we have all *had* parents—or parent surrogates—in our life. And certainly we have all *seen* parents in action. The father who browbeats his children into submission—demanding perfection, orchestrating their lives, criticizing and repatterning every minute detail of their characters—maintains control but does not help them develop personal responsibility. The mother who lets her kids run wild—offering no correction or guidance, giving them no time or attention—extends freedom to them, but does not help them learn boundaries or personal discipline.

True love balances correction with responsibility, freedom with boundaries, guidance with grace. True love allows for growth, for development, for increasing autonomy as the child matures. True love leaves room for mistakes without condemnation, space for exploration, freedom to fail. And when failure comes, true love corrects gently and sets the child upright to try again.

Good parents guide, direct, discipline, offer freedom,

and allow their offspring to find their own way. Above all, they love, and keep on loving.

Could the Almighty do less for the children of God's heart?

Becoming Adults of God

"I know what it means to be a child of God," one woman said concerning her own spiritual journey. "I want to find out what it means to be an adult of God."

I understood what she meant.

When I was in graduate school, I went home for a weekend to talk to my parents about an important decision I was facing. Some Christians in my religious circle, very certain that they knew exactly what God's will was for me, were trying to persuade me to give up my degree program and pursue a different course for my life. I felt trapped, and, frankly, I was looking for an out.

My father, an infuriatingly perceptive man, wouldn't buy into my program for self-justification. "You've always made your own decisions," he said flatly. "We've raised you to take responsibility for yourself. And now you want *me* to make your decision for you, to give you a ready-made excuse to say no? Forget it. We will love and encourage you, and whatever decision you make, we will support you. But you're an adult, and the ball is in your court, not mine."

Dad was right, of course. He usually is—he would tell you so himself, with a little provocation. But on this occasion, he knew I was attempting to avoid some important issues—taking responsibility for my own decisions, standing up to people who were trying to manipulate me in the name of Christ, looking to my own relationship with God rather than to someone else's "revelation" of God's direction for me. And Dad wouldn't let me get away with it. He insisted that I act like an adult of God.

In short, he loved me.

Had I made a poor decision and regretted it later, my father wouldn't have said, "I told you so." He wouldn't have condemned me for doing something stupid. He would have helped me get back on my feet—and then released me again to follow my own path.

I believe that is the way God deals with us as spiritual offspring. Throughout our spiritual infancy, childhood, and adolescence, we learn to evaluate right and wrong, to distinguish good from evil . . . or good from better. We "practice righteousness," master the basics of spiritual life, see them worked out in our everyday experience. We grow in an understanding of God's character.

And gradually, over time, the reins of control slacken. The way becomes less clear, the directing hand less forceful. God's Voice, which once resounded in our ears, now comes in whispers. And sometimes God is silent altogether.

It's tough to become an adult of God.

It's scary.

There are times, honestly, when we'd just rather have somebody go ahead and make the decisions on our behalf—to let us off the hook. After all, it's nice to have somebody else to blame when things don't go quite so well.

But is it really so important that we do everything

perfectly? Is the Lord so concerned that we "get it right". . . or is God more interested in the kind of people we are becoming?

On the Gunflint Trail near the north shore of Lake Superior, a group called Adventurous Christians has established a primitive camp. Here people come for winter retreats in February, for cross-country ski treks, for rock-climbing expeditions and canoe trips and dogsled outings. Except in the main lodge, there is no electricity, no running water, no central heat, no air-conditioning. Only the challenge to push yourself to the limit, to find out who you are on the inside. Being the best — climbing the highest, skiing the farthest, sledding the fastest — is not the goal. The point is not "doing it right"; the point is discovering yourself . . . your gifts and limitations, your inner longings and directions.

In Second Peter, the apostle gives us a startling and encouraging evaluation of our development as adults of God. Peter says, "His divine power has given us everything we need for life and godliness through our knowledge of him who called us" (2 Peter 1:3).

We have been given everything we need. We have been taught and disciplined, loved and chastened, directed along the path, and shown the faithfulness of the One who leads us.

We are equipped. We need only live out what has already been formed in us.

The journey of the spirit into the unknown is an "Adventurous Christian" outing of the heart and soul . . . the chance to challenge your preconceived notions, to explore your inner heights and depths, to expand your mind, to heighten your awareness of spiritual reality.

The One who called you out is not a dictator or a watchmaker. You are not expected to perform flawlessly, nor are you left entirely on your own.

Your soul is prepared for the journey, and your traveling companion stands by your side.

Take a deep breath, and rise to the challenge.

You have been well equipped.

The road beckons to you.

Walk on, adult of God.

CHAPTER FIFTEEN

The Burden of Being Right

The only hope, or else despair
Lies in the choice of pyre or pyre —
To be redeemed from fire by fire.
　　—T. S. ELIOT

Last evening a friend and I drove out to the country to see a new baby and take the mother out to dinner. Well . . . my friend was driving. I was preoccupied with reading, and I wasn't paying much attention.

As country roads will do, this one made several turns and twists. My friend had only been there once or twice, and she wasn't quite sure of the route. When we reached an intersection, she asked, "Left or right?"

I glanced up distractedly. "Either way," I said, and went back to my book.

The car didn't move. We sat there, idling, until I looked up and found her glaring at me.

"Which way?" she insisted.

I laughed. "Either way. It doesn't matter."

Obviously it mattered to her, because she waited

at the stop sign until I made a decision. Either road would have taken us to our destination. But in her mind, there was a right way and a wrong way to go, and she wanted to make sure she wasn't going the wrong way.

In our spiritual life, too, we sometimes respond with confusion, even anger, when we ask for directions and are told, "Either way." Conditioned by our family or religious upbringing, we often believe that life—especially life in the Spirit—is either right or wrong, black or white, left or right.

And no matter what the cost, we want to be right.

A couple of my friends have birthdays in February, and recently I went to the local card shop to look for birthday cards. I got sidetracked browsing among the Valentine's Day offerings, and I was intrigued by one in particular.

If loving you is wrong, I don't want to be right, the front of the card proclaimed. I flipped it open, and then began to laugh. *Of course I want to be right,* the inside text read. *I always want to be right.*

It's true of most of us, if we're honest. We always want to be right.

Right about our theology.

Right about our life choices.

Right about the way we raise our kids, about the music we listen to and the movies we watch—or don't watch. Right about the way we arrange the furniture and hang the pictures on the walls.

Right about . . . everything.

ONE WAY?

In the small town of Port Gibson, Mississippi, stands a church with a pitched roof and a tall steeple—an ordinary little church, to all appearances. Until you look up. At the top of the steeple, where you would expect to see a cross, sits a giant hand, its great golden forefinger pointing toward the heavens. Pointing, we assume, to God.

Back in the late sixties, when I came to an awareness of spiritual reality, this same symbol—a hand upraised with an index finger pointing to the sky—became the outward and visible sign of faith, a kind of secret handshake, a code that identified other like-minded believers. It was the signal of the Jesus generation.

Later the symbolism of the gesture became codified, organized into a nationwide campaign among Christians—the One Way movement. Thousands of churchgoers took up the gauntlet and began to wear their evangelism on their bumpers, while the uninitiated started to wonder if every city street in America had, overnight, been changed to a one-way thoroughfare.

One way.

It's a catchy slogan. Easy to spell. Easy to accept. No questions, no problems, no doubts. No wrong turns. No unmarked roads. No need for maps. Just a streamlined one-way street to your celestial destination.

The problem is, it doesn't work.

There isn't just "one way." Not even for Christians. The answers are never that simple.

"But wait a minute!" someone will protest. "Jesus said, 'I am the way.' What about that?"

Well, you've got me there. Jesus *did* say "I am the way" (John 14:6). He also said he is the truth, the life, the gate, and the shepherd (John 14:6; 10:9, 14). But if we want more than slogans as the foundation for our relationship with God, we must ask the all-important question: "What does that *mean?*"

What does it mean that "Jesus is the way"? As Christians, certainly, we believe that the sacrificial death and resurrection of Christ are the key and cornerstone of our salvation . . . that apart from Christ we cannot come into the presence of God. But how do we come? Is there *one way,* one "right way" that works?

Do I have to be sprinkled as an infant . . . or immersed as an adult? Do I come down the aisle to kneel at an altar, or stand to my feet at the conclusion of an evangelistic crusade, or raise my hand — one, or both? — when the call is given? Does the decision to follow Christ "take" more effectively in church than in my car during rush-hour traffic? Is it possible to grow into this faith from childhood, or is it better if I live a reprobate life in my youth so I'll have something interesting to tell at testimony time?

And if my way is the "right" way, what about all those poor misguided souls who haven't had the benefit of the same experience?

The dilemma about how we come into relationship with God is magnified a thousandfold when we begin to consider the infinite number of options open to us in the ongoing journey of faith. If there is one right way to come to God, then there must be one right way to live out the commitment — on the mission field, perhaps, or in parish ministry. Certainly some kind of "professional Christianity" is in order if we want to find the "one right way" to serve God.

How about prayer? Contemplation? Worship? Application of the Scriptures to everyday life? Service to others? Is there "one way" to do these things that negates the validity of all other ways?

And what of the thousands upon thousands of "little" choices we must make along the way in our journey with God? Is there a "right way" and a "wrong way" at every intersection? Does every crossroad carry with it the promise of everlasting bliss or the threat of eternal destruction?

"Hold on!" you say. "This 'one way' stuff is getting ridiculous. If God created us all as unique individuals, then isn't there room in God's plan for our distinctive personalities? If we all have to follow the same path, we'll end up like robots, little clones of one another. Besides, having to be *right* all the time is a terrible burden. . . ."

Now you're getting the idea.

Being right *is* a burden . . . an impossible weight, too heavy for the human soul to bear.

And yet God gives us choices. God does not always tell which way we should choose, which path we should select. Sometimes—increasingly, as we mature in faith and wisdom—the decision is left to us. And there may not always be "one right way" to go.

Do What Is in Your Heart

When I was a child—and to this day, if truth be told—I was fascinated with the kind of puzzles popular in children's magazines . . . those mazes where you're supposed to help the hero find his way from point *A* to point *B* without running into dead ends. Even as an adult, I have been known to sit in a restaurant and work the maze on the children's placemat while waiting for my pizza to arrive.

And early on, I discovered a trick. If you start from the end of the maze instead of the beginning, it's easier to find the right way. Somehow the path is clearer when you begin from the perspective of the outcome. It was cheating, probably, but it worked.

For generations, the debate over "finding the will of God" has raged. Some believers hold to the principle that God has a specific plan for each of us, and that the process of growing in faith is a kind of divine labyrinth, a celestial puzzle strung with booby traps. There's a right way and a wrong way. The right way gets you to point *B* in record time. The wrong way gives you false leads that leave you frustrated, face up against an impenetrable wall.

Those who accept the "holy maze" theory contend that every decision of the believer's life is fraught with eternal significance . . . the choice between darkness and light, between life and death.

But others—perhaps those who have tried the labyrinth method and discovered its limitations—have sought a more grace-oriented way.

In 1 Samuel 14, the warriors of Israel were facing their most dreaded foes—the Philistines. They had no weapons, and the outcome of the confrontation looked dismal. But Jonathan, King Saul's son, was not content to let the Philistines mock God. He made a decision . . . in light of

the circumstances, a pretty foolhardy decision. He took
his armor bearer with him and went out to face the Philis-
tine troops.

There is no indication in the Scriptures that Jonathan
was led by any clear direction from the Lord. He simply
did what he thought was right, and trusted God. "Come,"
he said to his armor bearer, "let us cross over . . . ; perhaps the Lord will work for us, for the Lord is not
restrained to save by many or by few."

And his armor bearer responded, "Do all that is in
your heart. . . . I am with you according to your desire"
(1 Samuel 14:6-7, NASB).

Do what is in your heart.

The presumption, of course — and it is an important
presumption — was that *Jonathan loved God and wanted
to do God's will.* With that as a given, Jonathan could
make decisions based on the need of the moment without having to search for a sign from heaven.

So can we.

The will of God is not a maze set before us by a celestial Being who delights in tricking us. There are, of
course, certain divinely established moral principles by
which we are called to live. But within those principles,
based on the foundation of love for God, we are free to
make our own choices . . . and to trust God for the outcome.

Garry Friesen, in *Decision Making and the Will of God*,
puts it this way:

> The *major point* is this: God does not have an ideal,
> detailed life-plan uniquely designed for each believer

that must be discovered in order to make correct decisions. . . . If the believer is free to choose, he is also *required* to choose. If there is no divinely determined "right" choice that the Christian must find in order to make a decision, then it follows that he may not shift the responsibility for the decision or its consequences onto someone else. Responsibility presupposes accountability.*

The "love God, and do what is in your heart" approach to decision making, however, is not always the easier way. Sometimes it seems less complicated to believe that God does have one right way in mind, and that our job is to find it and follow it. Then, at least, once we think we are on the right path, we can relax, because you can't go wrong in the center of God's will.

But life doesn't work that simply.

The reality is, God expects us to choose — not once, but over and over again. The Lord gives us, as we grow, increasing responsibility . . . and calls us to increasing accountability. And that spectrum that is designated as "the will of God" is not a tiny black bull's-eye on a target, but a vast, broad realm of possibility involving innumerable choices, all of which could be "God's will" for our life. We must decide for ourselves the way we will go: whether to marry or remain single, what kind of occupation to pursue, where to live, and what standard of living we will adopt. We take risks . . . and live with the consequences.

*Garry Friesen, *Decision Making and the Will of God* (Portland, Oreg.: Multnomah Press, 1980), 145, 181.

And we come, at some point, to realize that the actual choices we make may not be as crucial as the focus of our heart.

Loving God is more important than being right.

EITHER ROUTE WILL GET YOU THERE

One night, on a television game show, I watched an interesting variation on the "maze" principle. The show was based on competition between dogs . . . household pets the contestants had brought to the program. Part of the challenge presented to an exuberant two-year-old Irish setter was the running of a maze—through tunnels and water hazards, down blind alleys and past a dish of dog food—encouraged only by the voice commands of his owner, who was hidden behind a screen at the end of the run.

This Irish setter, confused by the insistent voice of his owner and frustrated by the dead end before him, finally just gave up and hurdled the barrier. He avoided the whole problem by making up his own rules. With tail wagging and tongue flopping, he dashed into his master's arms and gave the man a sloppy dog-kiss, then sat down, looking immensely pleased with himself. He lost the competition, of course, but he got where he was going.

Sometimes I think we might be better off to adopt the "Irish setter" approach to spiritual journeying: *Leap over the maze and get back to the master.*

Does it matter so much, after all, that we find the most direct route to our supposed destination? Isn't the real purpose to walk in love and trust with the One who has called us out?

Life in the Spirit is not a contest to see who can finish first, or fastest, or with the fewest diversions. It is not a labyrinth of wrong choices with a multitude of dead ends and only one right way to go.

Having to be right is a terrible burden. But the spiritual journey is not a test; it is a relationship.

Either route will get you there.

Either way will bring its own joys and challenges to the adventure.

The scenery will be different along the way, depending upon the choices you make. Some roads will lead through high mountain passes with bracing clean air and pristine snowfalls. Others will pass through valleys lush with greenery, or through deserts stark with a barren beauty.

You are called to choose your own path. But the One who has called you walks beside you on the way.

Vault over the barriers and embrace the Master.

Love God, and do what is in your heart.

Your road will lead you where you need to be.

PART SIX

Deep into Darkness

Before long, the way grew dense and rough. To their right, the low woods receded into a swamp, and clouds of mosquitoes hovered across the path. Thorns on the gnarled branches to the left ripped Quester's sleeve and drew blood from her upper arm. The muddy road narrowed to a single footpath, and soon Quester realized that her companion was not beside her.

"Guardian!" She whirled around, peering into the descending gloom behind her. He was nowhere to be seen. "Where are you, Guardian?"

Don't be afraid, came a low Voice from the mists. *I am here. Keep going, my Child; there is much you have not seen.*

"Guardian, is this the right path? Should we turn back?"

This is the way you have chosen. The Voice grew quieter until it was no more than a whisper. *Whenever we choose a way, the path closes up behind us. We cannot turn back; once the choice is made, the other paths no longer exist. We will walk through. There is much you have not seen.*

Quester strained again to see him, trying to hear his words, but the Voice faded into silence. Had he spoken, or had she merely imagined what she wanted to hear? Either way, she had no other alternative. She plodded on.

The path kept narrowing until at last it merged with the swamp itself, and so she slogged through knee-deep muck, swatting at gnats and mosquitoes and stopping periodically to pull leeches from the backs of her knees. As the sun climbed higher, the heat increased until Quester thought she would faint from thirst and fatigue.

"Guardian?" she called tentatively, flinging a leech into the thick brush. "Are you still there?" She squinted behind her, trying to make out his form, but she could see nothing. And this time no Voice came; only the croaking of bullfrogs and the whine of insects.

Quester's heart sank. *He is gone! I chose the wrong path, and he has left me to myself!* But about one thing Guardian had been right: There was no longer any path behind her; she had no choice but to go forward. She scooped up a handful of the fetid water, sipped at it, and spit it out. Then, sighing deeply, she wrenched one foot from the mire that sucked at her shoes and forced herself to move forward.

As the afternoon light began to fade, at last the swamp began to recede; the muddy water went down from her knees to her ankles, and finally she struggled out of the bog onto a narrow but recognizable path. She took a few exhausted steps into the shade of a large oak tree, collapsed against the trunk and, with her head on her knees, wept.

CHAPTER SIXTEEN

Blame, Shame, and Despair

Midwinter spring is its own season . . .
A glare that is blindness in the early afternoon,
And glow more intense than blaze of branch, or brazier,
Stirs the dumb spirit: no wind, but pentecostal fire
In the dark time of the year. Between melting and freezing
The soul's sap quivers.
   —T. S. ELIOT

It snowed again last night.

We had a week of reprieve—balmy, forty-degree days that melted the mountains of snow banked up from the plows. The sun came out. People smiled. Hope was reborn.

Then it hit us again. An Alberta Clipper sailed in from the Canadian tundra, bringing a thirty-degree temperature drop and a northeasterly blow that plummeted the windchills to nearly twenty below. This morning, instead of awakening to sunshine and birdsong, we heard the growl and scrape of snowplows and opened our eyes to another grim, gray Minnesota winter day.

We all knew it couldn't last, of course. In this part of the country, spring in February is a pleasant but hopeless dream.

Welcome to reality.

Shake out your coat and button up for another month or two.

Spiritual life, like the changes of the weather, moves in cycles. Sometimes we get an unexpected spring day—or week—in the middle of winter. We hope, sometimes desperately, that this time it will last. And when the gray clouds close in again, when darkness rolls in across our soul, we are tempted to give in to despair.

You choose a path . . . according to the best information you have, and with much prayer and deliberation, you make a decision. When you set out, the way seems clearly laid out before you. The sun is shining. It's a beautiful day for adventure.

Then the clouds begin to close in.

The promising company with the high-paying career—the one you built your whole future around—goes bankrupt, and you are left with a mortgage you can't pay for on a bigger house than you'll ever need.

You planned carefully for your retirement, only to find that the bottom has dropped out of your "sure" investment because of plummeting interest rates.

You spend five years and thousands of dollars and finally get your college degree, only to discover that a field that was wide open five years ago now has no positions available.

You buy a new car—the twenty-thousand-dollar model you've wanted for years—and on the second day, you back into a light pole at the mall.

The washing machine overflows.

The water heater rusts out.

The roof over your new sofa springs a leak.

Your dog bites the Mary Kay lady.

All on the same day.

Or, in less dramatic terms, you just keep slogging along, not feeling anything, questioning what happened to your sense of spiritual direction, wondering what became of the glory on the mountain.

Wondering if you made the right decision.

Wondering if anybody cares.

Even God.

Especially God. . . .

SECOND GUESSES

We live in a world of second guesses . . . people making changes, reconsidering, altering direction according to the circumstances. When things get difficult, we automatically assume that we made the wrong decision in the first place. So we back up, look around, and strike out on a different heading.

If the marriage is rocky, dump it and make a fresh start with a new spouse.

If the job is too hard or the boss too demanding, quit.

If the church doesn't respond to every immediate need, find a new one.

Shop around.

Punch the buttons on that remote control.

There has to be a better channel somewhere . . . greener grass . . . a more pleasant path.

If this way I've chosen is too arduous, then I must have made a mistake, picked the wrong one. This spiri-

tual journeying stuff is supposed to be fun . . . uplifting
. . . encouraging. . . .

Isn't it?

Not necessarily.

Sadly, the religious community has often fostered
the idea that walking with God is intended to be a
comfortable jaunt through flower-strewn pathways,
a cruise to ever lovelier spiritual realms of glory and
gratification.

We are told, to our detriment, that if something seems
wrong, if things aren't going the way we expected, we've
somehow missed the will of God. If we're sick or sad or
frustrated or feeling far from the Lord, there must be sin
in our life that needs to be confessed. If we wonder if
we've taken a wrong turn, we're instructed to go back to
where we began and reevaluate.

*Did you pray about it — long and hard, with fervency and
fasting and fleeces? No? Well, then, there's your problem.*

Were you sure — really sure — that this was what
God had told you to do when you made your decision?
What Scriptures did you base your choice on? What did
God say?

Heaven help us if we respond, "Well, God didn't say
much of anything, really. And I don't have any specific
Scripture . . . I couldn't find anything in the Bible about
taking this new job and moving to Minnesota. I evalu-
ated my situation, and it just seemed like the right thing
to do."

*Oh, my. No Scripture? No word from God? What an unspiri-
tual way to make a decision. God always gives us specific leading . . . if we are willing to be led. . . .*

The implication is clear. If I'm having trouble—if I'm doubting my choice, or looking in vain for some sign of the path, or feeling abandoned—it's my fault.

It has to be *somebody's* fault, after all. And only the really brave among us blame God: *The Lord didn't give me specific instructions. I can't be expected to make right choices without some direction. I asked, but I didn't get an answer. So, God, what are you going to do about it?*

Most of us, however, aren't quite that courageous. We blame ourselves instead, and wallow in shame and self-recrimination over our unspiritual approach to life choices. *I didn't wait for the sign. I got on the wrong road, and now I need to go back and start over. I'm a terrible person; God must be very disappointed in me. And look how much time and energy I've wasted traveling down this wrong path. . . .*

This approach to God's direction in our life reminds me a little of a game I play on the computer—a geography/culture intrigue called *Where in the World Is Carmen Sandiego?* I am the detective, and I have to track down the international criminal Carmen (or one of her henchmen) by following geographical and cultural clues that take me around the world. But if I choose wrongly . . . if I pick the wrong city as Carmen's next destination, I lose valuable time having to go back to the previous city to pick up more evidence.

The Lord's leading in our life, however, is not a cat-and-mouse game, a competition where God tries to trick us and we try to outwit or outmaneuver the Almighty.

The One who called us out never promised us an easy road or a detailed map to our destination. But the Lord's guidance is not a hoax. It's not some great celestial prank.

God's not trying to trick us. And we need to be careful about second-guessing God . . . or ourselves.

The reality is that sometimes, in this life, we just bog down. Sometimes things get a little more difficult or a little less clear than we had anticipated. Sometimes we choose a path, only to find that it narrows and disappears farther down the track.

But does that mean we made the wrong choice in the first place?

Is it possible that God has something else in mind altogether?

SECOND CHANCES

The Bible is full of stories about people who got a second chance . . . not a second chance, necessarily, to go back and make the "right" decision, but a second chance to trust God and find the grace and love of God in their difficult circumstances. These are the chronicles of hope, tales that show us the love and mercy of the Lord, and the opportunity God gives us to see the power of the Almighty at work in the lives of flawed, struggling people—people just like us.

Take Ruth, for example. She could have decided that she had made a poor decision in the first place when she married into an Israelite family. Things didn't turn out so well, after all. Her husband died, as did his brother and father, and Ruth was left with nothing . . . except a relationship with a bitter, heartbroken mother-in-law.

She could have gone home.

Orpah, her sister-in-law, did.

Naomi encouraged Ruth to return to the house of her mother. There she would have a chance to find another husband and make a life in her own country.

But Ruth made an unorthodox, unheard-of decision.

She chose to stay with her mother-in-law, to return to Israel with her, to adopt the lifestyle, customs, and worship of a foreign people.

Did she make a wrong decision in returning with Naomi to Bethlehem? She might have wondered, given the circumstances. In Moab, surely, her life would have been easier. At least she would have been among friends and family. Instead, she left everything familiar and chose a life of poverty and hardship.

Ruth was faithful to the path that was set before her. She committed herself to the decision and didn't second-guess God.

And God gave her a second chance.

Not a second chance to reevaluate her path and return home, but an opportunity to see the faithfulness of the God of Israel displayed abundantly toward her. Ruth didn't know it when she set out on the difficult road of faithfulness, but something important was waiting for her in Bethlehem.

A God who loved her.

A husband.

A life.

A future that destined Ruth, a foreigner, to become mother to a line of kings. Her great-grandson David turned out to be the greatest earthly king in the history of Israel. And generations later, Ruth's ancestral line traced down to the long-awaited Messiah, Jesus the

Christ, whose sacrificial death gave new significance to the prophecy spoken at the birth of her son:

> Praise be to the Lord, who this day has not left you without a kinsman-redeemer. May he become famous throughout Israel! He will renew your life. (Ruth 4:14-15)

Ruth had no idea her life would turn out this way. She just continued on the path set before her, even when she had no idea where it would lead.

It's easy enough, of course, to see God's grace in hindsight, to look behind us and realize that, no matter how difficult the path, it has been the right way all along. It is a different matter to trust when we do not know the outcome.

Still, that is exactly what we are called to do.

We are asked to make an adult decision, to launch out, to choose a direction based on the best information we are given.

But we don't have to second-guess every decision just because the way grows steep and rocky.

We don't need to blame ourselves—or God—when things get tough.

We don't have to grovel in shame and question ourselves at every turn.

We don't need to give in to despair when we can't immediately see the outcome of our choices.

We simply need to trust.

The One who called you out has led you this far. Sometimes the journey is lovely, filled with discovery and

wonder. Sometimes the way seems ominous and frightening. Sometimes, when you choose a way, the path closes
up behind you so that you couldn't go back that way
even if you tried.

But Guardian has promised to be with you—even
when you no longer see him or hear his Voice.

Amid winter storms or springtime's glory, at noon or
midnight, in darkness or in light, you are not left alone.

Do you think, just because things are difficult, that
you've taken the wrong path? Do you conclude that the
way would be less arduous if you had chosen another
road? Or is it conceivable that God has something else in
mind for you besides an easy way . . . something more
fulfilling, and ultimately more enduring?

Keep your eyes on the larger picture. Good things are
happening. You are growing, learning, going deeper. You
are moving from static religion to dynamic reality.

You are becoming the person God has called you to be.
And the struggle, the doubt, the questioning, are part of
that process.

Don't turn back now.

Endure the darkness. Bundle up against the cold.

A legacy may await you—a grander plan than you
could ever have imagined. Up ahead, just around the
next bend.

CHAPTER SEVENTEEN

The Invisible Presence

I said to my soul, be still, and wait without hope
For hope would be hope for the wrong thing; wait
  without love
For love would be love of the wrong thing; there is yet faith
But the faith and the love and the hope are all in the waiting.
—T. S. ELIOT

You remember Harvey.

Harvey, in the classic film by the same name, is the six-foot-tall invisible rabbit who accompanies Elwood P. Dowd (played by Jimmy Stewart) through a series of fantastic misadventures and hilarious misunderstandings.

Dowd is a gentle, unassuming soul. His relationship with his best friend Harvey brings him delight and fulfillment. But Dowd's stuffed-shirt friends and family try to have him committed—they are positive he is certifiably insane . . . just because he talks to an invisible rabbit.

It's a delightful farce. But it's also a significant commentary about the relative nature of sanity. By the time the movie ends, we are convinced that Dowd is the only character in the entire film who has a grip on reality. Because Harvey *is* real, even though we can't see him.

Isn't he?

Or did we just imagine him?

The world around us—sometimes even the religious community— often responds to us the way Elwood P. Dowd's unbelieving family reacted to his unconventional friendship with an invisible rabbit. We take risks, make changes, seek to go deeper in spiritual understanding. And people call us eccentric . . . fanatic . . . deceived . . . disturbed. They think we have lost our mind.

Sometimes we think so, too.

When we first set out upon this quest, we feel very certain that we have been called to leave the safe places behind and give ourselves to the adventure. Then things begin to go wrong.

We're not as sure as we once were that the One we follow knows where we're going. The way grows difficult and dark. We are compelled to make decisions we'd rather not get involved in.

And then, just when it seems we most need a reassuring voice, everything gets disturbingly quiet.

Our Guardian seems to vanish . . . or at least turn invisible.

And we're not so certain, after all, that having Harvey for a best friend is such a good idea.

Let's face reality. No matter what religious experts may say, sometimes God does seem to evaporate into the mists of our confusion and struggle. We suspect that we have been tricked, led into the wilds only to be forsaken. Or we blame ourselves: We chose the wrong path, and God finally just got fed up with us.

What do we do when God disappears?

How do we interpret the silence?

WHEN GOD IS SILENT

Certainly, God has a reputation for being present in the world, for intervening in the circumstances that affect us. After all, God did say, "I will never leave you or forsake you" (Hebrews 13:5, NRSV); "underneath are the everlasting arms" (Deuteronomy 33:27); and "no one can snatch [us] out of [the] Father's hand" (John 10:29). All these principles are true, of course, both biblically and experientially. God does protect us, hold us, cherish us, remain faithful to us.

But sometimes God is also silent toward us.

Some Christians would argue this point, saying that God does not pull away from us—that we are somehow incapable of hearing the Voice or sensing the Presence. But the Bible clearly indicates that God *does*, at various times and for reasons we do not always comprehend, withdraw from us and keep silent.

The prophet Hosea, for example, indicates that sin separates people from God. "Their deeds do not permit them to return to their God. . . . When they go with their flocks and herds to seek the Lord, they will not find him; he has withdrawn himself from them" (Hosea 5:4-6). Similarly, Isaiah indicates that rebellion against God causes the Lord to pull back: "When you spread out your hands in prayer, I will hide my eyes from you; even if you offer many prayers, I will not listen" (Isaiah 1:15).

But sometimes God is also silent when we have not sinned. Job, the great biblical example of the righteous person, bemoans the elusiveness of God's presence: "If only I knew where to find him; if only I could go to his dwelling! . . . But if I go to the east, he is not there; if I go to the west, I do not find him. When he is at work in the north, I do not see him; when he turns to the south, I catch no glimpse of him. . . . Why must those who know him look in vain?" (Job 23:3-9; 24:1).

Throughout the Psalms, David speaks of his own experience of God's silence: "Why, O Lord, do you stand far off? Why do you hide yourself in times of trouble?" (Psalm 10:1). "How long, O Lord? Will you forget me forever? How long will you hide your face from me?" (Psalm 13:1). And in the great Christ-Psalm, which Jesus cried out on the cross, the psalmist laments: "My God, my God, why have you forsaken me? Why are you so far from saving me, so far from the words of my groaning? O my God, I cry out by day, but you do not answer" (Psalm 22:1-2).

For four long, dark years—shortly after I had made a major life decision—I experienced such a withdrawing of the Lord's presence. I "looked in vain" for a glimpse of God. I confessed my sin, but the heaviness in my spirit remained. I prayed, but my prayers echoed back at me from an unresponsive heaven. I sought the Living Word in the pages of the Scriptures, but to my heart the Word was lifeless . . . a corpse composed of inapplicable principles and unfulfilled promises.

I wasn't used to this, and frankly, I didn't think it was

very fair. Throughout my spiritual life, I had been accustomed to a close, intimate, ongoing communication with my Lord. I was doing my part . . . why wasn't God responding?

I felt rejected, abandoned.

Well-meaning Christians told me, in effect, that it was my fault. If God seemed far away, I was the one who had moved. But no matter what I did, I couldn't get close again.

I felt like Quester in the parable: I had chosen the path based on the best information I had at the time. Had I made a wrong choice? Had the Lord forsaken me because I had somehow gotten out of "the center of God's will"?

After a while I got angry. *I'm doing my best to follow,* I thought, grinding my teeth. *Doesn't God have some responsibility in this, too?* And I remembered, ironically, Lois Lane's classic line in the movie *Superman*: "That's the problem with a Man of Steel . . . he's never around when you really need him."

I suppose we've all felt that way, but I didn't know it at the time. I was sure I was the only person who had ever harbored such feelings. And I felt guilty about feeling this way. I blamed myself. I blamed God.

Then, like the soft caress of a spring breeze, I began to remember something else.

When I was growing up, my father and mother insisted that I learn to take responsibility for myself. When I faced a difficult problem or decision, they didn't give me all the answers, neatly packaged with a label that read, *This is what you should do.* Sometimes they said nothing at all, but

waited patiently, giving me time to work out my own con-
clusions.

They were there, supporting me and encouraging me . . .
but they were silent.

Invisible, yet loving.

Believing in me.

Trusting me.

Giving me the leeway to succeed or fail on my own.

Children who have all their decisions made for them
never grow up, never learn to take on the responsibility
of being adults in their own world. Sometimes we need to
be left alone, to learn to tie our own shoes, to do our own
laundry, to negotiate that first frightening contract on a
new house, to grapple with a difficult decision. We experience frustration, self-doubt, even anger . . . but we learn.

Similarly, in our relationship with God, in our exploration of new spiritual dimensions, perhaps we need times
of aloneness, times in which our faith can be strengthened by walking in darkness for a while.

Luci Shaw describes the reality of the darkness as she
grappled with the death of her husband:

> I battled to know my God real in the dark while
> living in his silence, in the sense of his absence. Now
> and then lightning forked from the sky, like a mysti-
> cal sword, or a watery sun gleamed from the earth's
> edge. Sometimes I felt a glimmering of spirit like a
> clear night in the country, away from the artificial
> city brightness, the whole sweep of sky like a star
> map, with the constellations not just pricks of light
> but three-dimensional—near stars and far. . . .

But mostly it was a long darkness, like a sentence of death.[*]

We don't much like the idea of being "in the dark." The very concept has been given a negative connotation, implying not only the absence of light but the presence of evil. After all, we are called "children of the light" and exhorted to "walk in the light."

Yet reality teaches us that often our spiritual journey *is* a walk in the dark—not the darkness of evil and worldliness, but a walk of faith without the benefit of sight. The darkness and the light may both be alike to God, but they seem very different to us.

It doesn't seem fair.

Still, we are called to walk on.

With or without the benefit of light.

With or without understanding of the way.

Harvey is invisible, but he is still real.

That's what faith is.

FAITH AND SIGHT

As I journeyed through my four years of silence, gradually—not all at once, but almost imperceptibly, like sunrise on a cloudy day—a new truth began to dawn in my soul. I began to realize that, even though I missed having a conscious sense of God's presence and longed for a restoration of the closeness, my faith was taking on a new dimension. I learned to depend more on what I *knew* of God's character and goodness, rather than on what I *felt*.

[*]Luci Shaw, *God in the Dark* (Grand Rapids, Mich.: Zondervan Publishing Company, 1989), 13–14.

I began to lean on *grace* instead of relying upon my own ability to control my circumstances. And I discovered that my Lord had not abandoned me; God was still very much present in my life even when the awareness of that presence was hidden from me.

In other words, I was learning to trust God rather than trusting my perceptions of God.

The Scriptures teach us that "we walk by faith, not by sight" (2 Corinthians 5:7, KJV). We nobly—even righteously—declare that we don't need to *see* God act on our behalf in order to believe in him. We turn up our noses at poor old Thomas, who longed for visible evidence of the miracle of the Resurrection. We pat ourselves on the back and quote the appropriate verse: "Blessed are those who have not seen and yet have believed" (John 20:29).

Yet we who are so self-righteous about believing without the benefit of a sign nevertheless cling to a sense of the divine presence as a kind of security blanket, keeping ourselves

comforted by God's nearness and direction. The Bible defines faith as "the evidence of things not seen," (Hebrews 11:1, KJV). But often our desperate need to hear God's Voice, to sense God's closeness, to watch God's Word spring to life in our hands, is merely a transference, a different kind of *seeing*.

We want to be certain.

We want to hear a voice behind us saying, "This way."

We want to feel the warm comfort of our Guardian's nearness as we make our way into unmapped territory.

We want other people's affirmation.

In short, we want Harvey to stop being invisible. We

want assurances, so that we can say to others—and to ourselves—"See? I told you he was real. I knew he was still here. See? I'm not wrong, after all."

But God is a spirit.

And spirits are invisible.

EMBRACING THE INVISIBLE

Experiencing the nearness of God, feeling the Lord's pleasure in us, brings a wonderful sense of intimacy in our relationship with the Almighty—a joining that Scripture likens to the physical union between two people who love each other. But just as true love does not diminish with the absence of the beloved, our relationship with God is not jeopardized by the times in which God is silent.

In C. S. Lewis's *The Screwtape Letters*, the master demon Screwtape offers a staggering insight into the nature of God and his purpose for those who believe. Training his young nephew Wormwood in the fine art of undermining faith, Screwtape writes:

> Our cause [i.e., the cause of evil] is never more in danger than when a human, no longer desiring, but still intending, to do our Enemy's [God's] will, looks round upon a universe from which every trace of Him seems to have vanished, and asks why he has been forsaken, and still obeys.*

True faith, the faith that remains unshakable when all

*C. S. Lewis, *The Screwtape Letters* (New York: Macmillan, 1961), 39.

else is shaken, cannot lie in what we see, in what we feel, in what we sense. It must have its roots in what we *know*.

We know we were called out.

We know we have been led to this place.

We know God has called us to choose.

We know we want to follow.

We have responded with a holy yes to the summons to go deeper in the faith, to break new ground, to give ourselves wholeheartedly to the search. Now the question is:

Can we trust what we know when we no longer hear the Voice?

Can we have faith in a God who has become invisible?

The silence of God, the dark night of the soul that tries us to the very core of our spiritual depth, can become for us the catalyst to more genuine conviction. In the days of darkness, the nights of silence, we discover the true nature of our faith and the true faithfulness of our God.

As we launch out into deeper spiritual waters, we need to realize that times of silence are inevitable. God will use these sightless seasons in our life to deepen our true faith—a faith that cannot be shaken by the winds of change or undermined by the lack of the Lord's immediate presence.

You were not mistaken.

You have not lost touch with reality.

You were called, led, nurtured, and fed.

Your Guardian is real, even though invisible.

God is present, even when silent.

When the time is right, you will see again.

Press on.

CHAPTER EIGHTEEN

Surrendering to the Night

In the uncertain hour before the morning
Near the end of interminable night
At the recurrent end of the unending . . .
History is now . . .
With the drawing of this Love and the voice of this Calling.
  —T. S. ELIOT

In the blackness of midnight, the house creaks and groans as it shifts. The wind howls around the chimney, and a loose shutter bangs against the siding. Someone is rustling in the bushes just beyond the window. Monsters lurk underneath the bed.

The clock ticks slowly through the endless, sleepless night, marking the heartbeat of a terrified child, stretching out the time until the first gray light of dawn.

We are conditioned from infancy to fear the dark.

American poet Robert Frost captures this universal anxiety associated with darkness:

When the wind works against us in the dark,
And pelts with snow
The lower chamber window on the east,
And whispers with a sort of stifled bark,
The beast,
"Come out! Come out!"—
It costs no inward struggle not to go.[*]

As adults, we scoff at the idea of being fearful of the dark. We tell our children, "There's nothing under the bed. The darkness can't hurt you. Go to sleep."

We're brave.

We know there's nothing to be frightened of.

Darkness is perfectly natural, part of the order of the universe, part of the cycle of the earth's movement.

Being scared of the dark is for babies.

We're not afraid.

Or are we?

Is it possible that we are terrified of a different kind of darkness?

TWO REALMS OF DARKNESS

When we are called out of our safe places to walk into the unknown realms of spiritual exploration, we may suddenly find ourselves afraid of the dark—not the physical darkness that frightened us as children, but the spiritual sightlessness that often accompanies a new path. This is the unknown road, the spiritual midnight of our soul, those moments—or days or weeks or even years—

[*]Robert Frost, "Storm Fear," in *Collected Poems of Robert Frost* (Garden City, N.Y.: Garden City Publishing Co., Inc., 1942), 13.

when we cannot see the trail ahead, when the Voice of
the One who called us out can be heard no more.

God seems invisible—or at least silent.

We can't see where we're going.

We think we've lost our way, or chosen the wrong path.

Light fades, and darkness closes in.

And we are afraid.

But why?

Why are we afraid of the dark . . . those black nights of
the soul when nothing seems real, when our faith is
tried—and sometimes found wanting?

I think it's because we misunderstand the nature of the
darkness.

Like little children who imagine monsters under their
beds, we automatically assume that spiritual darkness is
innately evil. We remember some very graphic—and sometimes frightening—verses that condemn the darkness:

> Light has come into the world, but men loved dark-
> ness instead of light because their deeds were evil.
> (John 3:19)

> Walk while you have the light, before darkness over-
> takes you. (John 12:35)

> Let us put aside the deeds of darkness and put on
> the armor of light. (Romans 13:12)

> [God] will bring to light what is hidden in darkness.
> (1 Corinthians 4:5)

> What fellowship can light have with darkness?
> (2 Corinthians 6:14)

> You are all sons of the light and sons of the day.
> We do not belong to the night or to the darkness.
> (1 Thessalonians 5:5)

> God is light; in him there is no darkness at all. (1 John 1:5)

From these and other Scriptures, we get the impression that darkness *always* equates with evil, and light with good. If we're "in the dark," then, we must be in sin . . . we must have gone the wrong way . . . there must be something terribly wicked about us.

We want someone to turn on the light.

We want to see.

We desperately need to understand, to have answers.

And if we have no understanding, no answers, we try to formulate some of our own — anything to get us back into the light.

Some of us are so afraid of the darkness that we never launch out in the first place. People around us warn us to be careful. We are treading on slippery ground, pushing the envelope, dancing on the cliff's edge. This spiritual journeying can be dangerous stuff.

We might, after all, make a mistake. We might get lost. We might seem — or feel — unspiritual, unconnected with God. We might have to grow a little.

The Scripture does, of course, use images of darkness to represent evil and sin in our life. But there are other kinds of darkness that we face as we journey into the unknown — sightlessness that is related not to sin, but to spiritual deepening.

In the spiritual life, if we desire to move out into

new and uncharted territory, we have to be willing
to enter into a different kind of darkness, "the dark
night of the soul." This is not the darkness of sin or
separation from God, but the experience of "unknowing."

The fourteenth-century mystics understood the concept of spiritual darkness. The anonymous author of "The
Cloud of Unknowing" wrote:

> *When I first begin to reach out to you, my God,*
> *all that I find is a darkness,*
> *a sort of cloud of unknowing;*
> *I cannot tell what it is,*
> *except I experience in my will*
> *a simple reaching out to you, Lord God.*
> *This darkness is always between me and my God,*
> *no matter what I do. . . .*
> *If I am to experience you*
> *or to see you at all,*
> *insofar as this is possible here,*
> *it must always be in this cloud*
> *and in this darkness.**

We are slow to recognize this spiritual truth, however, slow to surrender to the darkness and embrace the
unknowing. The biblical writers warned us: Solomon
said that "the Lord has said that he would dwell in a
dark cloud" (1 Kings 8:12). Moses went to meet the
Lord on the mountain, and there God spoke "from out
of the fire, the cloud and the deep darkness" (Deutero-

---

*"The Cloud of Unknowing," in *Praying with the English Mystics,* ed. Jenny
Robertson (London: Triangle Books, 1990), 69.

nomy 5:22). The psalmists described the Lord as One who "made darkness his covering. . . . Clouds and thick darkness surround him" (Psalm 18:11; 97:2).

God dwells in darkness, as surely as God dwells in light.

But we don't relish the idea one bit.

We think we must fathom everything, so we're baffled and confused by our inability to comprehend.

We are so accustomed to seeing that darkness unnerves us.

We are so intent upon *knowing* that we cannot get comfortable with *unknowing.*

And so, in Dylan Thomas's words, we "rage against the dying of the light." We resist entering into the holy sanctuary of God's hiddenness. We struggle to see, to know, to understand.

We're afraid of the spiritual darkness.

LIVING IN HOLY SATURDAY

I remember a time of darkness in my own journey . . . a dark night of the soul that left me wondering where my path was leading, whether I was going anywhere at all, and if anybody cared—even God.

It was nearly two years ago, yet it could have been yesterday, the memory of it is so vivid. Sightless and nearly hopeless, I was wandering around in the Scriptures and in various other sources, not even knowing what I was looking for.

Then, almost by accident, the truth leaped out at me from the pages of a borrowed book, startling me with a clarity of vision I hardly knew was possible:

And then I knew — Holy Saturday — that's my place! That's where I'm living now — yes, yes, I fit here — it is familiar — that dry, empty place where color leaves the eye, music leaves the air, salt leaves the food, import leaves the word, lilt leaves the step — and what is left, what is left? Does despair live here also — that black hole of nothingness that is so engulfing on the Good Fridays? No, thank God, I don't see despair living here in Holy Saturday — And what is here in its stead, to fill up its empty space? . . .

And then, there in the corner, I spied her, sitting so quietly, yet with a certain dignity and strength about her — Hope sits there in the corner in place of black despair — She sits quietly, unobtrusively, because her thoughts are elsewhere — remembering the other Easter Sundays, the other Resurrection days.[*]

I recognized myself in those words. I, too, was living in Holy Saturday — the place of darkness, the waiting place, inside the tomb. I was biding my time until Easter, waiting in the dark for Resurrection morning.

And with that flash of insight, I discovered a vitally important truth.

I was not alone in the darkness.

Someone was in the tomb with me.

Jesus was there.

Walter Hilton, in "The Ladder of Perfection," puts it this way:

[*]Sarah Hall Maney, "The Space Between," in *Walking in Two Worlds: Women's Spiritual Paths* (St. Cloud, Minn: North Star Press), 95–96.

Jesus, you are both love and light,
and you are in the darkness
whether it brings pain or peace.
You are at work in my soul.
You move me to anguish
with desire and longing
for your light,

but as yet you do not allow me
to rest in your love,
nor do you show me your light.
This state is darkness,
because you have hidden my soul
*from the false light of the world.**

The darkness is not a threat to us. We do not have to fear it, seek to escape it, or let it bring us to despair.

We can embrace the night. For God is there with us.

GROWING BY NIGHT

Jesus told the parable, but sometimes we miss the whole point:

"This is what the kingdom of God is like. A man scatters seed on the ground. Night and day, whether he sleeps or gets up, the seed sprouts and grows, though he does not know how. All by itself the soil produces grain—first the stalk, then the head, then the full kernel in the head." (Mark 4:26-28)

*Walter Hilton, "The Ladder of Perfection," in *Praying with the English Mystics*, 70.

The seed grows *by night* as well as *by day*.

Darkness—the kind of spiritual night that comes upon us when we are seeking to go deeper in our relationship with God and our understanding of spiritual reality— does not negate the truth of God's presence with us. Like the man who sowed the seeds, we don't know how it happens . . . only that the dark night of the soul purifies our faith and gives us a more lasting hope, a more genuine trust.

Faith without sight.

Trust without comprehension.

Love without explanation.

When you enter the times of darkness and are tempted to give in to despair; when you feel yourself pressed in on every side by struggles and anxieties; when you wonder where the path leads—or if there is a path at all—consider the words of Rainer Maria Rilke:

> You have had many sadnesses, large ones, which passed. And you say that even this passing was difficult and upsetting for you. But please, ask yourself whether those large sadnesses haven't rather gone right *through* you. Perhaps many things inside you have been transformed; perhaps somewhere, someplace deep inside your being, you have undergone important changes while you were sad. . . .
>
> If only it were possible for us to see farther than our knowledge reaches, and even a little beyond the out-works of our presentiment, perhaps we would

bear our sadnesses with greater trust than we have in our joys. For they are the moments when something new has entered us, something unknown; our feelings grow mute in shy embarrassment, everything in us withdraws, a silence arises, and the new experience, which no one knows, stands in the midst of it all and says nothing.*

And remember . . .
Holy Saturday comes before Easter morning.
Night precedes dawn.
Darkness is part of the journey, too.
And God is there—in the tomb, in the darkness, in the silence; close, reminding you: "I will give you the treasures of darkness, riches stored in secret places, so that you may know that I am the Lord . . . who summons you by name" (Isaiah 45:3).

Surrender to the dark night of the soul.
Embrace your spirit's midnight, and be brave.
The darkness holds its own treasures, riches unknown to the day.
Wait with patience, and with hope.
Morning is on its way.
And when the dawn breaks, you will be stronger, ready to journey on . . . in darkness or in light.

*Rainer Maria Rilke, *Letters to a Young Poet,* trans. by Stephen Mitchell (New York: Random House, 1984) 81–83.

208

PART SEVEN

The Long Untraveled Road

She must have slept. When she awoke, the full moon had risen, and Quester thought she surely was dreaming—or else someone had transported her to another place and time. This could not be the horrible swamp she had come through! The moon shone silver on the water, and the night birds sang, swooping low over the rushes in search of food. The heat of the day had evaporated, and a cool breeze blew against her face.

Even before she heard his Voice, Quester sensed she was not alone. "Do you like what you see, my Child?"

Quester turned to find Guardian's shadowed form

sitting next to her, his back against the same tree. "Yes, Guardian, it is beautiful, but—"

"But what, my Child?"

The full force of Quester's exhaustion and confusion rose up in her. "Guardian, where were you? It—it has been terrible! The heat and the leeches and—"

"It was the path you chose, Quester."

"I know, Guardian, I chose it—you *made* me choose! And I chose the wrong path—" Quester sobbed uncontrollably, her breath coming in gulps, her voice breaking as she spoke. "I got myself into this, I admit, but you left me when I needed you most!"

Guardian took her hand and stroked it gently. "I never left you, Child—I was there with you, keeping the snakes and alligators at bay."

"I saw no snakes or alligators," Quester protested.

"There are many things in the swamp you did not see. You saw only what was needed."

"But I needed *you,* and I couldn't see you, or feel your presence with me. Why did you not speak to me?"

"Even for Guardians, Child, there is a time for silence."

Quester could not reply. She gripped his hand and cried until her tears were spent. He waited, and when her anguish abated, he put a hand beneath her chin and lifted her face to him.

"Quester, why do you think you chose the wrong path?"

She thought for a moment. "I suppose because I am stupid and inexperienced, and I was angry with you for speaking in riddles."

"But are you sure it *was* the wrong path?"

Quester exhaled loudly. "Certainly it was the wrong choice! If I had chosen the other road—"

"The way would have been easier, more pleasant?"

"Wouldn't it?"

"Perhaps," answered Guardian quietly. "Perhaps not."

Quester looked out over the beauty of the moonlit swamp and thought about his words. She said nothing, for there was nothing to say. At last Guardian's low Voice broke the silence.

"Quester," he said slowly, "you have discovered many new and wonderful things in the time we have walked together."

She hesitated. "Yes."

"What have you discovered here?" His arm swept in a broad arc, indicating the scene before them.

"Well—" She paused, groping for words. "I found that

I have more strength than I ever imagined, to come through the swamp alone."

"Quite true," he said. "It is a good thing to know."

"And," she continued, "now I see beauty that I never knew was here." She nodded toward the water as a heron glided in for a graceful landing in the shallows.

Guardian followed her gaze and smiled briefly, then turned toward her again.

"And I know," she concluded, "that I cannot go back the way I came."

The moon had set, and the light of dawn was pushing the shadows away. They sat in silence, shoulder to shoulder, and watched as the night creatures retreated to give place to the daylight inhabitants of the marsh.

Finally Guardian stood up and extended a hand to Quester. "There are many paths to walk," he said. "And there are others like you on the path."

Quester's eyes went wide, and she gaped at him, speechless.

"Did you think you were the only one on this journey, Child?" He laughed gently. "There are others — many, many others — who have left the safety of their fortresses and castles and ventured forth to walk with me."

212

"But where have they been?" Quester stammered. "And why have we not seen them?"

"Each travels his own path," Guardian replied. "And you needed to journey alone for a time. But there are places along the way where the paths draw near and cross. You shall meet some of your fellow travelers."

He smiled down at her. "Are you ready to go on?"

Quester did not ask their destination. Another question filled her mind. "Must I choose the way we take?" she asked.

"Yes," he answered simply. "Always."

She shrugged and reached up for his hand. "We cannot go back," she said. "So we will go forward."

She rose to her feet and turned in the direction Guardian was pointing. There, before her, stood a high stone wall, and in the middle of the wall, an open gate. She hadn't remembered its being there before. . . .

Something stirred deep in the recesses of her memory— an old, old dream, perhaps? With a sense of wonder she caressed the stones gently with her fingertips and put her hand to the bark of a gnarled old tree whose branches hung over the wall. It all seemed so familiar . . . the same, and yet not the same.

"Guardian . . . ?" she began. Then the question died on her lips and she looked into his eyes. He was smiling.

"Shall we go, my Child?" he asked in a whisper.

"Yes." A longing swelled within her heart . . . the desire to go farther, to draw closer to him, to understand more.

"Then come, Quester," Guardian said softly. "There is much you have not seen."

CHAPTER NINETEEN

Awakening, as from a Dream

The hint half guessed, the gift half understood,
is Incarnation.
　—T. S. ELIOT

I am a dreamer.

I dream of a log house on a peaceful lake, with a wide front porch that faces east. There, in the early mist of morning, I sit with my coffee and watch the sun rise, attending to the tranquil sounds of the woods coming to life, hearing the call of a loon on the far shore. I wait. I listen. And my soul is restored.

I dream of a society where prejudice and violence no longer exist, where people have the freedom to live and love and create and find fulfillment. I dream of a world where computers do what I want them to do, where music is soothing and meaningful, where kittens curl up in your lap and purr rather than tearing through the house breaking family heirlooms.

I dream of ballpoint pens that don't leave blobs of ink on the paper, of books that stay where I left them, of self-cleaning bathrooms and fat-free, sugar-free, cholesterol-free food that doesn't taste like the box it came in.

Utopia.

The perfect world.

Dream on. . . .

But pens clog up and books get lost and everything that tastes good is bad for me.

Welcome to reality.

The wake-up call has come.

THE DIFFICULT LIFE

M. Scott Peck begins his acclaimed book *The Road Less Traveled* with a profound, if obvious, truth: "Life is difficult."

Life is not easy—even spiritual life.

Especially spiritual life.

If we embark on the path of spiritual growth, seeking to move from religion to reality, with the assumption that things will be pretty simple, we are destined to be frustrated at every turn.

Religion is simple. Spiritual life is difficult.

When we give ourselves to religion, all we have to do is memorize the codebook. We learn—usually rather quickly—what is expected of us: how to act, how to dress, what to do and not to do, what key words will identify us as members of the elite. There is no real challenge here for inner transformation, no affirmation of risk, no encouragement to look beyond ourselves and find a different, more fulfilling way. There is, instead, a suspicion of new experience, an attempt to put the lid on individuality.

In religion, the goal is clear: we all look alike, talk alike, think alike. We are one. We know the right answers. We never have a dissenting vote on any decision. Isn't unity wonderful?

Spiritual exploration, on the other hand, is an intensely personal—and complex—way of life. It involves enormous risk, struggle, and sometimes heartache. It demands that we abandon our preconceived notions of God and the way God works, and learn to live with uncertainty and unanswered questions.

Spiritual life is difficult.

The journey is hard.

But it is worth giving your life to.

When I was a sophomore in high school—too many years ago to count—I had a Western Civ teacher named (honestly!) Hazel Ruff. Miss Ruff was the toughest old bird in the entire school system . . . and the best.

On the first day of class, Miss Ruff stood up and faced twenty-five trembling adolescents and said, "You have all heard of my reputation, I'm sure. You've heard that I eat sophomores for breakfast. Let me assure you . . ."

She paused, and the tension in the room closed in. She leaned over the podium and whispered, "Everything you have heard about me is true."

And it was.

Miss Ruff's class was the most difficult experience of my young life. I spent the entire semester terrified of giving the wrong answer. But I learned. And the *B* I earned from Hazel Ruff was worth an *A* from anyone else.

Irish poet William Butler Yeats wrote a poem entitled

217

"The Fascination of What's Difficult." In this poem, Yeats bemoans the fact that his calling—in this case, writing— is so difficult, and yet he cannot escape it:

> *The fascination of what's difficult*
> *Has dried the sap out of my veins, and rent*
> *Spontaneous joy and natural content*
> *Out of my heart. . . .*[*]

In the remainder of the poem, Yeats vows to quit writing altogether. It is too hard, too frustrating. And yet, until his death some twenty-nine years later, he continued to write, still giving himself wholeheartedly to "the fascination of what's difficult."

The difficult life of spiritual risk and exploration is like that. Sometimes we think it's just too hard, and we are tempted to give up and go back to the simple, predictable, comfortable life in the fortress-home behind the walled garden.

But once we really have a taste of the "fascination of what's difficult," we can't go home again. Oh, we could, technically. We could opt for the easier way. But it would never, never satisfy the hunger that has been awakened in us—the desire for a deeper, more intimate, more *real* relationship with the One who has called us out.

The Hard Is What Makes It Good

In the blockbuster comedy *A League of Their Own*, Dottie, the star catcher and hitter, decides to bail out on

*William Butler Yeats, "The Fascination of What's Difficult," in *Selected Poems and Two Plays* (New York: Collier Books, 1962), 33–34.

her team when her husband returns from World War II. She tells her coach, "I can't do it anymore. It's just too hard."

And the coach replies, "Of course it's hard. It's supposed to be hard. If it was easy, anybody could do it. The hard is what makes it good."

Consider your own life: spiritual, professional, personal. Chances are, the memorable times in your life, the experiences that brought growth and development, were the times of taking chances, of facing a difficult challenge and overcoming it.

Quitting a dead-end job and taking the risk to find more meaningful work.

Laboring for months—years, even—to overcome a thorny problem in your marriage.

Hanging in there with a rebellious teenager and finally rejoicing when he turns his life around.

Holding onto your faith through the dark night of the soul, and discovering at the end that God was not absent, after all.

These are the moments of glory, the times when all the difficulty, all the stress, all the struggle, all the pain, are transformed. . . .

And we realize that only the difficult stuff is really worthwhile.

Scott Peck says:

> Life is difficult.
>
> This is a great truth, one of the greatest truths. It is a great truth because once we truly see this truth,

we transcend it. Once we truly know that life is difficult—once we truly understand and accept it—then
life is no longer difficult. Because once it is accepted,
the fact that life is difficult no longer matters. . . .

What makes life difficult is that the process of confronting and solving problems is a painful one. . . .
And since life poses an endless series of problems,
life is always difficult and is full of pain as well as joy.

Yet it is in this whole process of meeting and solving problems that life has its meaning. . . . Problems
call forth our courage and our wisdom, indeed they
create our courage and our wisdom. It is only
because of problems that we grow mentally and spiritually.*

It's the hard that makes it good . . .
That makes it challenging . . .
That makes it worthwhile . . .
That makes it real. . . .

AWAKE AND ALIVE

In my daydreams, I may envision calm lakeshores
and a world of peace.

My night dreams are something else altogether.

Last night I dreamed of a many-tiered shopping mall
that went on forever . . . my personal vision of hell, no
doubt. If Dante had lived in the twentieth century, such a
mall would have found a place in the lower reaches of his

*M. Scott Peck, *The Road Less Traveled* (New York: Touchstone Books, 1978),
15–16.

Inferno, custom-made for those who hate shopping as much as I do.

At night, out of my subconscious arise visions of struggle—of climbing stairs and escaping danger, of searching for something—or someone—lost and alone, of dealing with the dark side of my own personality.

I awaken, but by the broad light of day, the struggle goes on. I still must climb and descend, journey through paths of light and darkness, search for the lost pieces of my soul, contend with my shadow . . . and take the risk to face reality.

And I remember Paul's exhortation: "Wake up, O sleeper, rise from the dead, and Christ will shine on you" (Ephesians 5:14).

Only when we awaken from the pleasant but innocuous dream of a stressless life, only when we open our eyes and acknowledge the difficulty of the journey, can Christ truly shine upon us.

For God is in the business of reality . . . the reality of leading us on a path that will challenge and strengthen us.

Yes, life is difficult.

But consider the alternatives. . . .

The only other option is death.

Jesus condemned the religious leaders of his day—the Pharisees, who considered themselves to be holy and above reproach, close to God—for their spiritual deadness. These were not the reprobates of society, the prostitutes and tax collectors . . . these were the elders and deacons, the Sunday school teachers and music directors—the people who kept the religious institution going. And to them Jesus said:

> Woe to you, teachers of the law and Pharisees, you
> hypocrites! You are like whitewashed tombs, which
> look beautiful on the outside but on the inside are
> full of dead men's bones. (Matthew 23:27)

"Choose life," Deuteronomy 30:19 commands. And we
smirk just a little, for who would be foolish enough to
choose death?

But people do it all the time.

When you're dead, you have no struggle or stress. You
have no battle with ongoing sin. You don't need to take
any more risks. You just lie there with your eyes closed
and let other people take over the business of living.

And it's not just the "unenlightened," the "unrepentant
sinners" who choose death. Many well-meaning religious
people give themselves over to spiritual deadening . . . to
the Novocain of the familiar, to the spiritual lobotomy of
a risk-free life. No brain, no pain.

It's easier, after all, just to stretch out on a satin cush-
ion. A corpse has no choices to make, no uphill battles to
face, no uncertainty to endure.

But eventually the coffin lid closes, the box is buried
six feet under, and decomposition begins.

Far better to stay awake, to keep our eyes open, to face
the struggles and challenges and difficulties that authentic spiritual life presents.

Far better to feel the pain and face it than to anesthetize
ourselves and become numb to the joy of the challenge.

Far better to live in reality.

Life is difficult, but the difficulties are transformed
when you acknowledge them.

No pain, no gain.

In the struggle lies your strength.

Awake, sleeper; rise from the dead. This is the journey into reality. The hard is what makes it good.

CHAPTER TWENTY

Epiphany

We shall not cease from exploration
And the end of all our exploring
Will be to arrive where we started
And know the place for the first time.
　　　—T. S. ELIOT

I remember the first time I saw my house.
It was a bleak, cold day in February, five years ago.
The house itself could have been described as bleak —
gray and weather-beaten, unoccupied for months. The
heat had been turned off, and I could see my breath as I
stood in the dining room and surveyed the tattered carpets and faded wallpaper.

There was an emptiness about the place, a longing to
be filled.

And so it was with my heart.

For years I had prayed for a place to belong . . . a spiritual home, where my soul could find nurturing and rest.
But here?

This couldn't be the place . . . this ancient, sagging

house with its vast expanse of dreary, vacant rooms, its scarred oak woodwork, its leaking front porch.

Could it?

I went away, looked at four more houses—all in better repair—and then returned. Once more I found myself wandering up the front staircase and down the back. I sat on a radiator and looked around. I shook my head in despair at the very thought of the enormous amount of work that would be necessary just for the place to be livable.

Then something happened.

My eyes were opened, and I began to see the possibilities. With some paint and wallpaper, carpets and love . . . and a good deal of effort . . .

Yes. This was it after all. God had plans for me here.

It was a moment of miracle. My heart had come home.

MAGIC EYES

In his wonderful book *Forgive and Forget*, Lewis Smedes tells "a little fable" of "The Magic Eyes." A man, deeply hurt by his wife's unfaithfulness, comes ultimately to the truth that will set him free from bitterness:

> There was one remedy . . . only one, for the hurt of wounded heart. . . . He would need eyes that could look back to the beginning. . . . Only a new way of looking at things through the magic eyes could heal the hurt flowing from the wounds of yesterday. . . .
>
> "Nothing can change the past," he said. . . .
>
> "Yes, poor hurting man, you are right," the angel said. "You cannot change the past, you can only heal

the hurt that comes to you from the past. And you
can heal it only with the vision of the magic eyes."*

Smedes uses the fable of "The Magic Eyes" to illustrate
a principle of forgiveness. For those of us who have journeyed through the darkness and finally come into a new
light, the concept applies as well to our understanding of
reality.

When Quester awakens after coming through the
swamp, everything seems to have changed. It is the same
scene, but different. The very environment that caused
her pain and despair now appears beautiful, illuminated
by moonlight.

She is not deceived. Rather, she sees with magic eyes.

In our journey, our walk of faith, a similar miracle happens to us. We resist the decisions that need to be made,
and we despair when we seem to have made the wrong
choice. But as we come through the difficult times, we discover that, even when he seemed invisible, our Guardian
has not left us. And we begin to see differently.

An acquaintance of mine has signed up at a nearby
university for a weekend "ropes course." The students
arrive in the morning, are strapped into a harness, and
spend the day climbing ropes to incredible heights.

It sounded perfectly horrible to me, but she was looking forward to it.

"When I face my fears—in this case, claustrophobia
and fear of heights—and overcome them, I feel better
about myself," she said. "I find that I am successful at

*Lewis Smedes, *Forgive and Forget* (San Francisco: Harper & Row, 1984), xiv.

something I never thought I'd be able to do. It's wonderful . . . really."

I wasn't quite convinced. But I understand the principle.

Going *through* the challenge is more fulfilling than finding a way *around* it.

You think you can never do it.

But once you're on the other side, you find yourself looking at the situation with different eyes. You see in a different light.

It's an epiphany . . . a moment of inspiration and illumination when we get a glimpse, a flash of truth . . . and we understand.

WHAT HAVE YOU DISCOVERED HERE?

In the final movement of the parable of Quester, Guardian asks an all-important question: "What have you discovered here?"

It's easy enough to talk about discovery and new light and insight when we're on the mountaintop basking in the glory. But it's far more difficult to accept the magic eyes to see beyond the pain and struggle, to discover the change and growth that happens in the darkness, when we cannot see or feel the progress.

I remember, years ago, catching a glimpse of the importance of resurrection—not just the physical resurrection of Christ on Easter morning, but also the many spiritual resurrections that God desired to accomplish in my own life.

I focused on that sliver of light and began to pray that the Lord would bring about resurrection in my life—in my work, in my spiritual understanding, in my relationships, in every area of my experience.

I knew not what I prayed for.

And I got much more than I bargained for.

Things began to fall apart. Relationships turned sour. My work suffered. My spiritual life entered the doldrums. Choices I had made in good faith led me into impossible complications. I felt as if God had reached down a hand and stirred up all the silt on the bottom of my fishbowl.

I cried. I prayed. I demanded an answer.

Then I went back and read the context of the Resurrection.

This glorious moment, the centerpiece of all spiritual life, was surrounded by pain and blood, betrayal and anguish, incomprehensible suffering, abandonment, and finally . . . death.

I wanted resurrection in my life.

But I wasn't so sure about all this other stuff.

I would have preferred simply to emerge from the open tomb in glory, like the movie star who steps into the end of an action scene after a stand-in has been beaten and bruised doing all the dangerous stunts.

The problem was, the "other stuff" was as much a part of the answer to my prayer as the glory of Easter morning.

My soul could not appear from behind the rolled-away stone in a pristine white robe, unbloodied by the Crucifixion. I had to stumble up the path to Golgotha, feel the weight of the cross on the torn skin of my back. I had to wait out the long night in the darkness of the tomb.

The Savior bore my sin, but I still had to live my life.

And that experience led me to an important moment of epiphany. God asked me, "What have you discovered here?"

And I was able to give an answer based on reality:
Resurrection is preceded by crucifixion.

Labor and blood accompany the process of birth.

Oddly enough, the revelation brought with it a sense
of liberty, an illumination that resulted in an unparalleled
freedom for my soul. My experience was not the exception, after all. The pain, the sense of betrayal and abandonment, the blood and sweat and tears of Gethsemane
were all part of the Resurrection package. Jesus had
experienced them, too.

I hadn't made wrong choices, after all.

I hadn't gone the wrong way.

I had to go *through,* to the other side of awareness.

And now I can see my pain with magic eyes.

THE MOMENT OF TRANSFORMATION

For those of us who grew up in a religious environment that led us to expect a peaceful and painless road,
reality may seem a dismal and discouraging prospect. But
when we can see through magic eyes, we discover a wonderful truth: that all of life's experiences are transformed
when we view them as part of the ongoing journey of intimacy with God.

The Bible gives us a clear understanding of this
principle . . . if we have eyes to see it. The writer of
Hebrews tells us, "No discipline seems pleasant at the
time, but painful. Later on, however, it produces a har-
vest of righteousness and peace for those who have been
trained by it" (Hebrews 12:11). And Paul says, "Our
present sufferings are not worth comparing with the
glory that will be revealed in us" (Romans 8:18).

This does not mean that we will *forget* the difficult times, but that they will be put into proper perspective . . . just as the agony of labor recedes in the joy of new birth. When our eyes are opened to reality, we see the nights of darkness and the days of glory as natural movements in the continuous rhythm of spiritual life. Even the swamp that threatened to overwhelm us takes on an ethereal beauty by the light of the risen moon.

The scene has not changed.

But we see it differently . . . with magic eyes.

C. S. Lewis, in *The Great Divorce*, gives a startling picture of what it means to interpret life with this kind of transformed vision:

> Heaven, once attained, will work backwards and turn even . . . agony into glory . . . [and] damnation will spread back and back . . . and contaminate even the pleasure of the sin. Both processes begin before death. The good man's past begins to change so that even his forgiven sins and remembered sorrows take on the quality of Heaven: the bad man's past already conforms to his badness and is filled only with dreariness. And that is why, at the end of all things . . . the Blessed will say, "We have never lived anywhere except in Heaven," and the Lost, "We were always in Hell." And both will speak truly.*

With the eyes of faith and the heart of trust, you can look beyond the sweat and the pain and the near despair

*C. S. Lewis, *The Great Divorce* (New York: Macmillan Publishing Co., 1946), 67–68.

of a difficult path. You can go forward, even when the One who called you out remains silent, invisible. For at the heart of the struggle lies an epiphany, a moment of transformation . . . not the transformation of your *circumstances*, but of your *seeing*.

You may not have all your questions answered.

You may never understand all the *whys*.

But Guardian is there . . . looking out for you, protecting you from unseen predators, and ultimately opening your eyes to the beauty and wonder inherent in an experience that you thought held only terror and frustration.

And what have you discovered here?

Perhaps the truth that crucifixion comes before resurrection, that labor precedes birth, that facing reality is more fulfilling than denial.

There is something familiar about this place, something that tugs at your soul. You have been here before . . . in your dreams, in your moments of longing.

It is not quite the way you imagined it, but this is the place of your victory. This is reality. This is home.

You have not picked the wrong path. The way you chose may bring challenge and difficulty, but it gives you the opportunity to be tested, to find out what you're made of.

You are braver than you thought you were.

And as you survey your circumstances with magic eyes, a wonderful transformation takes place.

You see beauty as well as danger.

You find courage in the awareness of your strength.

You discover that Guardian has not forsaken you.

And you are drawing closer to the One who called you out.

CHAPTER TWENTY-ONE

The End Is Where
We Start From

What we call the beginning is often the end
And to make an end is to make a beginning.
The end is where we start from.
　　—T. S. ELIOT

Real life is full of endings . . . partings . . .
farewells.

Some of those farewells are joyful, bittersweet occasions. . . .

Watching a six-year-old board the bus for the first day
of school. Packing the last kid off to college. Wiping
away tears as the bride and groom wave from the back-
seat of a departing car.

Other endings are more difficult. . . .

Saying good-bye at the deathbed of a parent. Signing
the final papers to dissolve a twenty-year marriage. Listening to the door slam as an angry teenager stalks away
into an unknown future.

There is, Ecclesiastes says, "a time for everything"

(Ecclesiastes 3:1). For beginnings and endings. For greetings and good-byes.

Sometimes we like the beginnings better. We'd rather hold onto them than give way for the natural ebb and flow of life—for maturing, growing, changing, separating . . . and eventually, dying.

Even in the spiritual realm, we would prefer to remain in the first holy bliss of discovery. But as we face reality, we learn that there are mountains to climb, deserts to cross, difficult challenges to face.

Seasons change. Children grow up. Parents grow old. Sooner or later, the last chapter of the book has to be written.

ENDINGS AND BEGINNINGS

My friend Jackie, who just turned thirty-one, recently gave birth to her first child . . . a delightful, miraculous little girl. As Jackie neared the end of her pregnancy, she declared—as most expectant mothers do—that she just wanted to "have it over with," to get this birth done and get on with her life.

When little Michela was born, we joked that Jackie was far from "over with it." She had, in fact, only begun. The end of the pregnancy would be just the beginning of motherhood—of nurturing and correcting, of teaching and comforting, of responsibility unlike anything she had ever known before.

In giving birth to her daughter, Jackie marked the end of one way of life and the beginning of another. She lost something—the freedom to pursue her education full time, the leisure for long conversations with friends, time to write and meditate and concentrate fully on the spiritual dimension of her life.

But she gained something, too. Something different, perhaps, in the challenges and demands of parenting. Something new, something totally unfamiliar.

It was an ending, and a new beginning. . . .

The end is where we start from.

Back in the late sixties, a popular poster sentiment proclaimed "Today is the first day of the rest of your life." The cynics among us edited the saying to read "Yesterday was the end of the first part of your life."

It all depends on your perspective.

But whether we see change as promise or threat, the reality is, life never stays the same. Relationships grow closer, or apart. The honeymoon weeks or months give way to the years of emotional commitment demanded by a marriage. Children grow up, rebel, form their own individual personalities. Kittens turn into cats. The paint on the garage begins to peel.

Things change.

And in our spiritual life, if we want to continue to grow in wisdom and intimacy with God, we need to embrace the changes. We need to learn to view the *ends* as new *beginnings.*

COMMENCEMENT DAY

I have been a graduate in four commencement ceremonies, a professor in six, and a spectator at several more. Without exception, the visiting speaker has commented on the nature of "commencement"—that is, the beginning of the new life that awaits the graduates in the great unlimited future before them.

Most of the graduates, however, view the ceremony as an end rather than a beginning . . . the end of term papers and tests and grappling with unreasonable professors; the end of early morning classes and institutional food and the pressure of constantly having to prove themselves. They wave diplomas in the air and shout, "I did it! I'm done!"

Those of us who have been there before them smile benignly and let them have their day of celebration. But we know. This is not the end. It is only the beginning.

If you thought you had to prove yourself in class, O Graduate, just wait until you face your fifteenth job interview. If you thought cafeteria food was bad, wait until you taste a microwave dinner. If you thought professors could be unreasonable . . . well, you haven't met your first boss yet.

But we don't tell them. They will learn it for themselves, soon enough.

And we might be wise, somewhere along the way, to apply that same principle of endings and beginnings to our spiritual quest for intimacy with God.

The journey, after all, is a succession of new beginnings. As we walk the path of spiritual reality, we move through cycles of light and darkness, of challenge and comfort, of glory and discouragement. There is a time to rest and a time to move on . . . but the journey never ends.

The prophet Elijah struggled with the concept of endings and beginnings. In the greatest challenge of his spiritual life, he faced the prophets of Baal on Mount Carmel. It was a spiritual battle unparalleled in biblical history.

The prophets of Baal set up their altar, prepared their

sacrifice, and began to call out to their god. All day, from early morning until noon and from noon until the time of the evening sacrifice, they prayed and prophesied and cut themselves with knives. But no one answered.

Then Elijah took the stage. He repaired the altar of the Lord, laid the wood and the carcass of a bull upon it, and stood aside. But he didn't pray — not yet. First he called for water, four large jars full, and poured it on the altar, drenching the sacrifice, the wood, the stones. Three times he soaked the sacrifice, until water ran down the altar and filled the trench on the ground below.

Finally Elijah stepped forward and offered up a simple prayer: "Let it be known, O Lord, that I am your servant and that you are God. . . ."

In a scene that would rival the drama of a Steven Spielberg film, the fire of the Lord fell upon the altar. It burned up the sacrifice, the wood, the stones, and the soil, and evaporated the water standing in the trench (1 Kings 18:20-39).

It was a great day of victory for the Lord . . . and for Elijah. The crowning moment of the prophet's career.

Good grief! How do you follow an act like that? Where do you go from there?

Elijah went into depression.

Jezebel, King Ahab's wife, had corrupted the king with idol worship and slaughtered the prophets of God. When she heard what Elijah had done, she put out the word that his name was next on her list. And Elijah, the great prophet whose God had come down in fire, ran to the wilderness, sat under a tree, and prayed to die.

"I have had enough, Lord," he said. "Take my life" (1 Kings 19:4).

Elijah didn't understand the cyclical nature of the journey. The moments of victory and majesty, the times of fear and darkness and silence, weave together in the intricate fabric of our life with God. After the magnificent victory occurs—the Olympic gold medal of spiritual challenge—we cannot simply bow out, retire, and fade quietly from the limelight. We cannot live in the afterglow of our glories.

Life goes on. The path stretches further ahead of us, up the high mountain and down into the deep valleys.

We have our victories, certainly. We have our moments on Mount Carmel, when God comes through in a blaze of fire and declares the power and presence of the Almighty. We can rejoice and be thankful when we slog through a dismal swamp and come out on the other side.

But this is not the culmination of the journey.

We have not arrived.

Every point of ending is a place of new beginning.

You have come a long, long way. You have left behind the battlements of religious sameness and launched into reality. You have seen truth and welcomed it. You have assumed responsibility for yourself, owned your own opinions, made decisions you thought you could never make.

You have discovered that even when he seems invisible, your Guardian has not left you. You have seen beauty where you once saw only pain and struggle. You have learned that the path leads forward, and that a difficult climb can be more fulfilling than an easy one.

You have embraced the challenge, and you are
stronger for it.

But this is not the end. It is only the beginning.

You are not at the same place you were when you
started.

You are not the same person.

You have changed, developed, matured, grown wiser.

Your experience in the darkness has strengthened your
faith, bolstered your trust in the One who called you out.

And now you are beginning again.

A new lane beckons.

A new way lies before you . . . another fortress-home
to leave behind, another garden gate to mark your
entrance into the ongoing path.

This is the commencement celebration of your soul.

There will be trying times ahead, no doubt—demanding passes through the cold and snow, dark nights of
uncertainty. But there will also be days of wonder and
discovery, new cliffs where you can stand and feel the
fresh wind in your face and look below to the vast
uncharted panorama of your future.

A day you've never lived before is dawning in the east.
The long untraveled road stretches out before you.

And a Voice is calling, whispering to your heart: *Come
out; there is much you have not seen.*

Becoming Real

Because some of us were raised in the church, where religious tradition can often get in the way of a truly intimate relationship with God, we occasionally get confused, in terms of our spiritual life, about what is real and what is not.

In this book, I have tried to encourage you to look beyond the traditional, well-established modes of religious perception to discover the reality of your own life with God. This does not mean that we have to throw out everything we've been taught — baby, bathwater, and all. But we do need to evaluate carefully the systematic expression of our religious faith, to find out not just what, but *why* we believe.

The process of becoming real, of leaving behind empty ritual and investigating for ourselves the reality of a God who loves us, is no easy task. Organized religion often condemns or resists such a search, because it challenges the carefully constructed superstructures of the status quo.

From a more charitable viewpoint, the religious community also wants to protect us—to guard us from ourselves, from the possible danger of looking in the wrong place for spiritual reality. It is a genuine concern.

But the bottom line is, God can be trusted to lead us.

And when we are willing to be led, we discover a whole new world of spiritual reality—a world where we don't have to deny or explain away the presence of darkness or struggle, a world where we can embrace and rejoice in the challenges that strengthen us.

One of the most profound books I have ever encountered on the subject of reality is not a "spiritual" book at all—it is a children's tale called *The Velveteen Rabbit.* In the story, the Velveteen Rabbit asks the wisest of all the nursery toys, the Skin Horse, about becoming Real.

> "What is REAL?" asked the Rabbit. . . ."Does it mean having things that buzz inside you and a stick-out handle?"
>
> "Real isn't how you are made," said the Skin Horse. "It's a thing that happens to you. When a child loves you for a long, long time, not just to play with, but REALLY loves you, then you become Real."
>
> "Does it hurt?" asked the Rabbit.

"Sometimes," said the Skin Horse, for he was always truthful. "When you are Real you don't mind being hurt."

"Does it happen all at once, like being wound up," he asked, "or bit by bit?"

"It doesn't happen all at once," said the Skin Horse. "You become. It takes a long time. That's why it doesn't often happen to people who break easily, or have sharp edges, or who have to be carefully kept. Generally, by the time you are Real, most of your hair has been loved off, and your eyes drop out and you get loose in the joints and very shabby. But these things don't matter at all, because once you are Real you can't be ugly, except to people who don't understand. . . . Once you are Real, you can't become unreal again. It lasts for always." *

Real isn't how you're made. It's what happens when you are loved.

For love is what draws you from religion to reality . . . the love of the One who called you out, whose name is Love. Love desires above all things to bring you into a relationship that is real — not based on superficialities or traditions, but on the experience of seeing faith work in your everyday life. Your own faith, not your parents' or your pastor's or your Sunday school teacher's . . . a faith forged in the refining fires of real human experience, out where you get battered and bruised by sin and struggle.

*Margery Williams, *The Velveteen Rabbit* (New York: Avon Books, 1975), 12–16.

Sometimes becoming real hurts.

But it hurts good.

Because once you're real, you can't become unreal again.

It lasts for always.

Additional Titles of Inspiration from Tyndale House Publishers

COME BEFORE WINTER AND SHARE MY HOPE
Charles R. Swindoll 0-8423-0477-0

A GOD TO CALL FATHER
Michael Phillips 0-8423-1392-5

ON THE ANVIL
Max Lucado 0-8423-4568-X

THE HIGHEST LIFE
Gene Edwards 0-8423-1351-6

THE INWARD JOURNEY
Gene Edwards 0-8423-1629-9

THE SECRET TO THE CHRISTIAN LIFE
Gene Edwards 0-8423-5916-8